SCOTT A.
BESSENECKER

HOW TO INHERIT THE EARTH

SUBMITTING OURSELVES TO A SERVANT SAVIOR

IVP Books

An imprint of InterVarsity Press
Downers Grove, Illinois

InterVarsity Press
P.O. Box 1400, Downers Grove, IL 60515-1426
World Wide Web: www.ivpress.com
E-mail: email@ivpress.com

InterVarsity Press® is the book-publishing division of InterVarsity Christian Fellowship/USA®, a movement of students and faculty active on campus at hundreds of universities, colleges and schools of nursing in the United States of America, and a member movement of the International Fellowship of Evangelical Students. For information about local and regional activities, write Public Relations Dept., InterVarsity Christian Fellowship/USA, 6400 Schroeder Rd., P.O. Box 7895, Madison, WI 53707-7895, or visit the IVCF website at <www.intervarsity.org>.

Scripture quotations, unless otherwise noted, are from the New Revised Standard Version of the Bible, *copyright 1989 by the Division of Christian Education of the National Council of the Churches of Christ in the USA. Used by permission. All rights reserved.*

Design: Cindy Kiple

Cover Images: iStockphoto
Interior images used by permission.

ISBN 978-0-8308-3728-1

Printed in the United States of America ∞

Library of Congress Cataloging-in-Publication Data

Bessenecker, Scott.
  How to inherit the earth: submitting ourselves to a servant savior
  / Scott Bessenecker
    p. cm.
  Includes bibliographical references.
  ISBN 978-0-8308-3728-1 (pbk.: alk. paper)
  1. Meekness. 2. Humility. 3. Submissiveness—Religious
aspects—Christianity. 4. Control (Psychology)—Religious
aspects—Christianity. I. Title.
BV4647.M3B47 2009
241'.4—dc22

                                                    2009031643

P 19 18 17 16 15 14 13 12 11 10 9 8 7 6 5 4 3 2 1

Y 24 23 22 21 20 19 18 17 16 15 14 13 12 11 10 09

To Hannah

CONTENTS

ACKNOWLEDGMENTS

Just after finishing the first draft of this work in the fall of 2008 I watched prairie grasses smoldering under a controlled burn at a Benedictine monastery where I often go to get alone with God. Prairie restoration involves rescuing some seeds from the prairie, then setting the grasses on fire with the objective of destroying the weeds and predatory plants and enriching the soil. The rescued seeds are replanted so that in the spring the prairie begins a new, more vibrant life.

I felt God say to me, "This is what I want to do with your book."

That was a bit discouraging to hear, but it was what the manuscript needed. The first draft of this book was discontinuous and rambling, so I invited some friends to harvest some of the seeds and help me burn it. Now, in 2009, I see some early shoots sprouting up from the ashes of the original. Without that controlled burn and replanting, you would definitely be holding something with more weeds and less beauty.

Dave Zimmerman, my editor, pressed me forward on this project when I debated whether I should write the book in the first place. Anyone who makes comments in the margins like, "Yummy! More of this" or, "This reads a little sterile, like you're holed up in your cubicle," displays a love affair with words and their power to move us. He also solicited feedback from readers who helped enrich the soil. Thanks for not taking a torch to it in an uncontrolled burn.

Work colleagues Jim and Beth Tebbe, Helyn Luisi-Mills and Jill Feldkamp gave sacrificially of their personal time to comb through the ramblings and help me determine what it was I really wanted to say. Justin Markofski and John David Pitts stirred me with their lives as much as with their comments on the manuscript. Lots of students, InterVarsity staff and my church family have all listened patiently to me wrestle with these ideas, and they asked questions which have really sharpened my thinking on the topics of meekness, submission, repentance, following, servanthood, obedience and real leadership.

Janine, my wife, who models so much of what I talk about in this work, and my kids, Hannah, Philip and Laura, who know how unmeek I can be, have borne with patient encouragement my writing, thinking and speaking on the topic. Sharing life together with you all has been such a wonderful tool to deepen my spiritual walk. Hannah, to whom this book is dedicated, has a passion for justice for those on the margins like very few others I know.

At one point in my writing I confessed to God that I did not want this to simply be a collection of my own impotent thoughts, but then again neither did I want to serve as God's keyboard, letting him write the book. I wanted this to be our work . . . together, a kind of father-son project. To the extent we achieved that collaboration, it is more a testament to his grace than to my yieldedness.

For those of you who find only charred remains and very little life in *How to Inherit the Earth*, set the book aside. Maybe if you pick it up a few years from now and look at it again you'll find something small growing.

ONE

SUBVERTING MONOPOLY™ THROUGH MEEKNESS

For Sale: Quaint Southeast Asian Country Priced to Sell."
I stepped into the ten-foot-by-ten-foot scrap wood shed on a hot
Phnom Penh afternoon. Bopha[1] lay dehydrated and ashen, fading in
and out of sleep on a bed of wood slats. Her baby, now five days old,
was sleeping next to her. This was child number seven. She had
delivered her in the shanty on Tuesday, cutting the umbilical cord
herself as she had no one to help. When my eyes adjusted to the
dark, I could see her husband, passed out on a hammock just two
feet from me. Child number one was gone. Bopha didn't know where,
probably one of the many street kids of Cambodia. Child number two
was "stolen," she said, which probably means she was sold or
abducted into the sex industry. The third child was about twelve; he
came in and out a couple of times during our visit. The fourth and fifth
children played about us, and child number six, hardly a year old, sat
naked next to his mother, pulling at her for attention. Bopha lifted her
head and looked at him in irritation for a moment, and then plopped it

back down on the wooden bed. Once or twice she vomited between the slats. Bopha, like her children, are casualties of MONOPOLY™.

MONOPOLY™ is that all-American game where the sole objective is to be the first person to buy up all available property, plot by plot, and then to charge such exorbitant rent that you drive each and every friend or family member in the game into utter financial ruin, until finally you have acquired all the money and all the property possible. Created at the height of the American Depression, it's easily one of the world's all-time most popular board games. How do we account for the fact that the theme of personal domination makes for such well-loved games? It's not just an American phenomenon either. The idea of lording over others is the essence of most games in most parts of the world. Could it be that one of our primal human instincts is titillated when we obtain utter mastery over others, even if it leads to their ruination? Are games that excite our desire for supremacy tapping into some kind of distorted version of the Genesis call from God for humans to "have dominion over . . . every living thing that moves upon the earth" (1:28)? Whatever the case, MONOPOLY™ has outsold all other board games of its kind with estimated sales of over 250 million copies. We all apparently love to rule over others.

This would be just a curious observation but for the fact that a real-life MONOPOLY™ game is going on in most of the world. Much of the property in cities of the developing world is either wholly owned by or under the control of powerful families (or the corporations the families own). Other property is under the control of the "government," which in some cases amounts to little more than a family-run business. For the world's poor, the MONOPOLY™ board has been set and the property has been doled out to others. They will live their entire lives paying rent to the few who own everything—and with wealth and power concentrated in the hands of a few comes the power to maintain domination for generations. Bopha and her community are suffering under the oppressive power of MONOPOLY™.

Honestly, I'm a bit ashamed to admit that I despaired of any hope for Bopha and her family. I wondered what it might be like to live in the conditions they endured day after day. Gambling and prostitution were probably among the most popular ways to earn money in this squatter settlement where families had no rights over the land they were living on. But gambling is no consistent way to bring home money, and prostitution probably contributed to the baby factory Bopha had become. Besides, if the little cash intake was being used to purchase alcohol, poverty's anesthesia, then what hope was there of any real, lasting change?

I suppose there is always the hope of conversion to Christianity. Buddhists believe a person is poor because they deserve to be, but in Christianity, we discover that all humans, no matter their station, are made in the image of God and have been redeemed at a great price. We then can experience a transformation of mindset. Unfortunately, I have known too many impoverished, drug-addicted Christians to be convinced that conversion alone would instantly heal the ills of this Cambodian family. For one thing, the family had few employable skills. But what if, along with conversion, Bopha and her husband received a basic education? In reality, early childhood malnutrition and years of "anesthesia" had likely rendered them partially learning disabled. Even with a university education or job training, double-digit unemployment in Phnom Penh means that some with university degrees are unable to find work.

But let's imagine for a moment that Bopha and her husband become Christians, stop drinking and gambling, and get trained to operate a sewing machine. By both working twelve-hour days in a sweatshop they may be able to scrape by. Nonetheless, accomplishing this feat would require a number of people helping for years just to get this family to the place of most poor Cambodians. It would mean somebody with patience and skill committing themselves to a long, trying period of three-steps-forward, two-steps-back progress. But even with this advance from desperate, intractable poverty all the way up to only bottom-rung poverty, Bopha and her family would likely never be able to own a small piece of property on which they could build a livable structure and pass along to their children. In fact, her community, Dey Krahorm, was being forcibly evicted and relocated to an undesirable area, far from city services and jobs.

The government of Cambodia is parceling up the land on which Bopha and her community live and selling it to the highest bidder. Developers are betting that the tourist industry in Cambodia will grow. As of April 2008, 45 percent of the land mass of Cambodia had been sold.[2] The poor (and the middle class, for that matter) have no real chance to purchase this land. Wealthy individuals and developers are not only able to come up with the cash required to purchase the property, they're also willing to pay for the prostitutes needed to "service" the government officials and the parties that will enable the sales to go through. The land on which Bopha's community is located was purchased by a local rich family who is clearing the land under the guise of "developing" the area. "Development" almost always spells bad news to the poor who are "developed" right off their land and tossed into even deeper poverty, their homes bulldozed with little to no compensation. Economists like Hernando de Soto Polar believe that without the ability to legally own a piece of property, the landless poor like Bopha and her children are destined to live in perpetual desperation.[3] They are locked out of MONOPOLY™ and serve only as income generators—"rent payers"—for those who own the board, until it becomes more convenient to kick them out.

Bopha's family is one of many thousands of dispossessed, impoverished families in the area. Add to this the reality that there are a billion squatters on the planet, and that they're growing at nearly three times the rate of general population growth, and you can appreciate my despair.

If the property of billions of people is in the hands of a few game-winners intoxicated by the idea of winning at all costs, where is the hope for those who have been born losers?

MEEKNESS: A COUNTERINTUITIVE ANSWER TO THE WORLD'S PROBLEMS

The hope for the world lies in meekness. Jesus said, "Blessed are the meek, for they will inherit the earth" (Matthew 5:5). The reason that the meek will inherit the earth is that they are naturally disposed to use power in the way it was designed by God to be used—as a guard for the weak and to preserve the common good—in contrast to those with MONOPOLY™ power, who consolidate wealth and status in a single set of hands at the expense of everyone else. Notice that the beatitude from Matthew 5 does not say that the meek will conquer the earth or take over the earth. They will inherit it. It's a trust given to them by their Father.

Wielding power with meekness is part of the design for humanity. It is the means by which the cosmos can operate most effectively. And for the person at peace with themselves and with God, meekness is a natural impulse, a quality which emerges because the ego is not hungry. But when we're insecure, when we fear the slippage of our position, our deeply engrained broken desires come to life, clamoring for money, status and power even if it means crushing those around us. As the apostle Paul said, "Those who want to be rich fall into temptation and are trapped by many senseless and harmful desires that plunge people into ruin and destruction. For the love of money is a root of all kinds of evil, and in their eagerness to be rich some have wandered away from the faith and pierced themselves with many pains" (1 Timothy 6:9-10).

Meekness is the state of the healthy human freed from those "senseless and harmful desires," freed from the fear of losing. The meek are able, like Jean Vanier and Henri Nouwen, to leave their jobs at the height of their careers to care for severely developmentally disabled adults. The meek will gravitate to those whom the world discards—whether the poor, the disabled, the homeless or the socially leprous—not simply out of compassion, but because they know there is much to learn from the broken. The meek are magnets for children because they are like children in some ways; they have that remarkable ability to embrace innocence without becoming ignorant of evil. Meekness comes when the soul is at rest, and when given power to rule the earth, the meek will create a dominion that will subvert the self-oriented MONOPOLY™ world. But becoming meek requires dying, which is why so few pursue meekness.

STARVING THE OLD SELF

When I think about the greedy developers in Cambodia and the corrupt government officials, I'm filled with indignation. But it is an indignation eager to judge others and very reluctant to judge self.

A Sunday school teacher once read to his class one of the parables told by Jesus in Luke 18. It's the story about a righteous Pharisee standing in prayer next to a corrupt tax collector. In the parable the Pharisee prays, "God, thanks that I'm not like this tax collector," and he proceeds to remind God of all the great things he's done. The tax collector, on the other hand, beats his breast and says, "God, be merciful to me, a sinner!" The point of the story was that the repentant and humble sinner walked away justified, while the arrogant, self-righteous, do-gooder did not.

Completely missing the point, the Sunday school teacher ended his class by praying, "God, thank you that we are not like this Pharisee!" The authors who recount this story joke that they had to suppress the desire to profess through their laughter, "God, thank you that we are not like this Sunday school teacher."[4]

I know myself well enough to recognize the resemblance between me and the developers or the Cambodian government officials. I cling to my money and sometimes scheme about how to use it as a magnet to get more. I can be jealous of those who excel at things I'm also good at, wanting to elevate my position in relation to them. I gravitate toward ruling over others and squirm under someone else's authority. These are forces at work in me and, if unchecked, they push me to exploit power at the expense of others in order to increase my position in the MONOPOLY™ game. But that will do me little good when the meek inherit the earth.

That tendency for followers of Jesus to succumb to the ways of this MONOPOLY™ world, giving up their inheritance in a kingdom where repentant sinners, poor people and unsophisticated children are at the top, and instead chasing after worldly pleasures through deceit, is referred to as the "old self" in the Bible (Ephesians 4:17-32; Colossians 3:1-17). Likewise, the Bible talks about the "new self" as that nature which faithfully resembles the God in whose image we were made, dominated by characteristics like meekness, love and the peace of Christ. The "new self" is the real picture of humanity without lust for supremacy over others. It is what we were meant to be.

I'm trying to kill the "old self," starving him of the things that feed his nature, and I'm attempting to revive the picture of God deposited in me by feeding those things true to my real nature. That's what this book is about. To do that we first have to journey into a lifestyle of meekness and downward mobility at the expense of pride (chapter two). If I'm serious about starving the old self, I must find ways to embrace a kind of submission born of love in a culture that prizes the exercise of authority and the exaltation of leadership (chapter three). This path I seek is an exploration into wealth-crippling acts of generosity brought on by real repentance which spins resources out to the thirsty edges of the world (chapter four). I'll need to examine the excellence of following without comparison (chapter five) and the beauty of embracing a slave mindset while destroying an attitude of entitlement (chapter six). Finally, I'll try to capture the beauty of obedience as pictured in monastic orders while helpfully undermining the independent spirit which leaves us fractured and alone (chapter seven). In short, this book is about subverting the game of MONOPOLY™ through the practice of meekness, and becoming the people we were designed to be from the beginning, when the world was new. When we discover that, then we'll be prepared to lead others into a new kind of kingdom (chapter eight).

THE SECRET RULES

What if there were secret rules to MONOPOLY™ hidden to the greedy, the arrogant and the power-hungry? What if things like giving away property, loaning money at low interest rates, redistributing property when things got too lopsided or lowering rent for those who couldn't afford to land on your space were actions that were recorded and honored? What if love and meekness could be measured and remembered, and all those who had lost the dog-eat-dog version of MONOPOLY™ or been ridiculed because of their servile attitude of submission were put in charge of a new iteration of the game?

The person hosting me and others in Bopha's squatter community in Phnom Penh was a young, Finnish, YWAM[5] missionary named Pia. She was bright and intelligent and could have been a "property owner" in most any earthly game she chose to play. Instead, she had spent years in this community, learning the language, developing friendships and telling others about Jesus' kingdom through her lifestyle as much as through her words.

Pia and friends

Pia introduced me to her friend Dara[6] who lives in the same dispossessed community. Dara glowed with excitement when she talked. "My favorite song is 'I Have Decided to Follow Jesus,'" she told me. "I love the part that says, 'the cross before me, the world behind me, no turning back. No turning back.'" Dara had given up gambling and her husband was beginning to climb out of his alcohol addiction. She is materially poor, but she is the "good soil" upon which a seed has fallen. Her submission to Christ is infectious, and I thoroughly believe that in the course of her life there will be a thirty-, sixty- or one-hundred-fold increase of other people like her. Her decision to put the cross before her and the world behind her will change things. Pia and Dara are quietly and humbly subverting MONOPOLY™. A church is formed, a community center established and the balance of power invisibly shifts.

I also met Chris on this trip. Chris works with InnerCHANGE, a

Christian order among the poor. He and his family live in simplicity among the poor in Phnom Penh, believing that wealth can become a power dynamic which inhibits their dependence on God and becomes a barrier in their relationships with the poor. Chris and InnerCHANGE are standing up to developers by planting themselves among poor families on the eve of their illegal eviction in order to amplify their cries for justice. Attention is brought to bear on inequities, land rights lawyers are retained, laws change, and slowly, over time a new kind of kingdom begins to take shape.

While in Phnom Penh, I also hung out with a group of people who work with Servants to Asia's Urban Poor (Servants). Servants' workers move into some of Asia's most desperate slums, living alongside slum dwellers and working with them as neighbors for kingdom change. The Servants community in Phnom Penh is made up of rich, poor, foreign and local believers all living in simplicity among the poor just as Christ came to dwell among the least. These men and women have founded a Khmer-led organization called TASK which is caring for AIDS patients, sex workers, disabled children and those left to rot on the margins. Working humbly, often flying under the radar of the power-brokers, a kingdom which esteems the outcast is taking root.

These are people who have learned the secret rules. They are living the reality of a kingdom more real than the kingdom of this world, which is passing away (1 Corinthians 7:29-31). They have taken the downward path, the path of service and meekness and submission. They know the secret about the coming reversal, where those at the bottom of the food chain are lifted up and those at the top are made low, and they live that reality today in the here and now as if the kingdom of God has come among us. And even though the way of meekness comes with its own set of troubles and hardships because it is both "here" and "not yet," they live it because they know it is the way things were meant to be, the way that *they* were meant to be. Living our design is less wearing on our souls, less wearing on the earth and less wearing on those around us. That's why it's important for us to discover this path and to set out on it. That's why I have written this book.

TWO

MEEKNESS AND
THE DEATH OF PRIDE

The *Collins Essential Thesaurus* ties the following
set of adjectives to the word *meek: spineless, weak, tame,
boneless, weak-kneed, spiritless, unresisting, wussy* and *wimpish*.
People exhibiting meekness are not exactly the sort of people you
expect to rule the world. But according to Jesus, the meek are
precisely the ones who will inherit the earth (Matthew 5:5), as we
saw in the last chapter. Jesus is actually quoting Psalm 37 in that
portion of his Sermon on the Mount:

> Be still before the LORD, and wait patiently for him;
>> do not fret over those who prosper in their way,
>> over those who carry out evil devices.
>
> Refrain from anger, and forsake wrath.
>> Do not fret—it leads only to evil.
> For the wicked shall be cut off,
>> but those who wait for the LORD shall inherit the land.

Yet a little while, and the wicked will be no more;
　　though you look diligently for their place,
　　　　they will not be there.
But the meek shall inherit the land,
　　and delight themselves in abundant prosperity.
(Psalm 37:7-11)

Rather than sniveling wussys, this psalm describes the meek as men and women of deep conviction who patiently bear up when the wicked prosper. Rather than lashing out in anger at those who do evil, they restrain themselves, waiting for the final chapter to begin when a great twist in the plot will take place. In his book on the Beatitudes, Dave Andrews says that the word *meek* in Jesus' day was used to describe someone who exhibited "quiet, controlled, internal strength of character, which opponents would interpret as a sign of weakness to their own peril."[1] The Hebrew word for "meek," *anayw,* is used synonymously with the word *humble* (Psalm 34:2) and even the word *poor* (Psalm 9:18). In fact, the great Isaiah 61 passage that Jesus uses as his inaugural address in Luke 4 ("The Spirit of the Lord is upon me, / because he has anointed me / to bring good news to the poor") is really a declaration that Jesus was appointed to bring good news to the *anayw*—the meek.

Poverty of spirit, humility, meekness . . . these are the sorts of character traits at play when a young, educated woman with most any lucrative profession before her chooses to quietly work in a Cambodian slum empowering the poor, while government officials and wealthy developers seem to be prospering in their conniving ways. The meek one is the poor woman living in a slum who has given up gambling and drinking because she's decided to follow Jesus. The cross of difficulty is before her and the temporary pleasures of this world are behind her. Still, she faces the powerlessness of her circumstances joyfully, without turning back.

The meek are those working for land rights for the poor, loaning them their voice and standing up to the powers-that-be at great personal cost. These are not spineless wimps. They are people of courage, full of peace in difficult days because they know something that the corrupt men and women in power do not know. Namely, that it is the meek, not the corrupt, who will inherit the earth.

A life lived in simplicity, humility and obscurity will be a very handy asset at the end of the game when God is looking for meek people to put in charge. The rich and famous who wield worldly power will be at a distinct disadvantage. Possessing disproportionate control in this world through the use of money, fame and power has a tendency to kill meekness in a person. I'm not saying you can't be rich, powerful, famous *and* meek. I'm just saying it's hard, like trying to push a camel through a needle's eye. The possessor of money, fame or power can easily slip into imagining himself or herself to be more important than those who do not possess such things, and try as they might to beat ego down, they find themselves tangled up in pride.

I've never really bumped into a famous person in my day-in, day-out existence. You know, the kind of thing where you run into Oprah at the mall. Once, however, I did sit next to a guy on a plane who was part of the sixties rock group The Turtles. They were the group that performed the 1967 hit "So Happy Together," which kicked the Beatles' "Penny Lane" out of the number one spot on the charts. During our flight from Los Angeles to Detroit, we struck up a great conversation. Turtle-man was a nice guy, a very interesting person to speak with. He told me how superstardom had really messed with his head. Apparently, being eighteen years old and touring the country with rock and roll celebrities of the day was the sort of stuff that bends your ego out of shape. I guess being turned into a god overnight had side effects he hadn't reckoned on. The band entered the fast lane of pop culture, and suffered heartbreaking, bitter fights with managers, record label people and band members that more or less destroyed their rising star trajectory.

At the end of the flight I remember thinking that he seemed nice enough for a not-recognizable-on-the-street-but-famous-enough kind of star, but I realized later that we had spent hours talking almost exclusively about him. Achieving real meekness will be difficult for this good man who has had more than forty years of excessive attention thrust upon him.

Many of us, I would wager, harbor some desire to be "famous," even within a limited circle of people. Facebook is a very popular social networking website, at least during this blip in history. I've gotten dozens of Facebook solicitations that say, "I can't believe it, forward this message and see who accesses your Facebook profile the most." It was tempting. I was curious to see who was looking at my profile because it makes me feel good to be sought out by others. Most of us like being pursued by people who really like us (unless there's a restraining order involved). While I resisted the temptation to forward that message, I do succumb to other vanities, like checking to see how many people visit my blog. (Please *do not* check out www.thenewfriars.com, lest you feed my fame-hungry ego. That website, again, is www.thenewfriars.com.) There's something about my sense of status that increases when I'm known and sought by others.

My desire to be known, loved and sought out is part of the ego-hungry tendency to measure success by increasing possessions, power and popularity—these are the age-old human desires. But these things are enemies of meekness. And if we want to enjoy real life and the transforming power of submission, we'll need to learn the art of meekness and welcome the death of pride.

STATUS, POWER AND WEALTH: GROWTH HORMONES FOR PRIDE

I would have to fight an inner sense of failure if I made less money next year than I did this year, or if I had fewer friends or wielded less influence in my neighborhood, church or workplace. Even if I stay the same, a feeling of failure rises up within me every time friends whom I view as peers advance beyond me in some way. Somehow I sense I'm made the lesser by their advancement. The meek, however, can celebrate the promotion of peers, even when those peers advance beyond their own place of worldly status.

When I was ten years old I lived in Australia. I had a friend named Richard who apparently was allowed to smoke—or so he told me. There was something status-boosting about smoking cigarettes at age ten. I was jealous that Richard could smoke and I couldn't; I felt so young in comparison, so immature. So one cold winter morning I decided to try to recover my lost status by somehow making Richard believe I could smoke too. I didn't want to really smoke, though, so I rolled a small pile of pepper, which seemed to me very much like tobacco, into a tube of paper. I figured since it was cold enough to see your breath, Richard would assume I was smoking if I were puffing on my pepper-filled tube.

I had the status-boost all worked out in my head. We had a veranda on our second floor; I would stroll out as Richard padded up to our house on his way to school. He'd say, "Hey mate, come on down, let's go to school," and I would casually take a drag off of my "cigarette" and say, "Just a sec, mate, whilst I finish up this cig." And I'd blow a mean cloud of smoke from the side of my mouth. Of course, my plan didn't work very well because I kept drawing in burning mouthfuls of pepper each time I took a drag.

Richard's status awakened pride in me. Pride is the opposite of meekness, as it is the foundation of most all sin and one of the few attitudes actually described as an abomination to God. Pride is rolling your eyes (even if only internally) at someone who says something you think is stupid, even if it is. It's insisting on the fact that you are right, even if you are. Pride is not necessarily the good feeling you get when you help someone; rather, it's the good feeling you get when you tell others about how you helped someone and then reimagine the good deed over and over in your mind. And pride is smoking a fake cigarette because you can't stand the fact that your friend can smoke but you can't.

Meekness is set against pride. Proverbs 16:19 says, "It is better to be of a lowly spirit among the poor [literally *meek*] / than to divide the spoil with the proud." To be in need and meek is of greater advantage to the godly than to be divvying up the winnings with successful conquerors. Meekness is listening for the kernel of truth in something stupid that somebody says. Moreoever, the meek do not have to be right all the time . . . even when they are. Meekness is helping a learning-disabled and somewhat cantankerous person do their grocery shopping and feeling as though you have just had the honor of spending an hour and a half with Jesus.

I usually don't think of myself as a very proud person. But then December rolls around—that time of year when I receive Christmas letters from friends, chronicling all the wonderful advances they and their children have made during the past twelve months. I almost always feel as though I've been demoted after reading them. So I begin trying to reinterpret my year in ways that brush aside my struggles and losses and inflate my successes. It's like standing out on the veranda drawing in burning mouthfuls of pepper in an effort to appear more sophisticated and successful than I really am. I prop up my acts of charity and successes and sweep under the carpet my self-serving attitudes and actions. I find ways to describe my job or my travels so that they sound more important than they really are.

One of the ways we measure ourselves against one another is

by the amount of power we possess. A CEO is generally considered to have greater status than a jobless person because the CEO has more power—the authority to control people, systems and money. The president of the United States, in turn, has even more status—more power—than CEOs. I'm sure most of the people who run for president are fine people. But chasing the U.S. presidency has at its root the aspiration for power—a desire to gain control over citizens, institutions and resources. It may be with benevolent designs, but it's *their* benevolent designs. Presidential contenders aren't interested in being anyone's puppet. They want to use political power to shape America and the world according to their notions of what is good and acceptable. Even the most saintly candidate will expend exorbitant amounts of money and energy in a bid for the White House, believing their plan to wield unbelievable power is better than their rivals'.

In some ways this drive for dominion is God-given. When God planted human beings in creation he intended for them to "subdue [the earth]," and "have dominion over" the things he had made (Genesis 1:28). Humans were his regents, stewards made in his image as ambassadors over creation. A person's desire to be in authority, then, is at least in part due to the fact that God has wired us that way; he created order and authority and intended for us to maintain order through the exercise of authority. If I seriously believed that all pursuit of power was evil I would live as a recluse in a cave somewhere, espousing anarchy as the only way for humans to live an unspoiled life.

Just as the acquisition of status can inflate pride and distort ego so can the acquisition of power. It is a growth hormone for pride and is toxic to meekness. In the fall of humankind, we were no longer satisfied to wield power as regents of God. We decided to wield power as gods ourselves, casting off the posture of ambassadors and adopting the posture of the King himself. Since that day, our ability to brandish power in meekness without succumbing to the lie that a human power-holder is little more than a steward of a great king, has become an immensely difficult task that few have accomplished flawlessly.

The desire for possessions or the tendency to measure ourselves by how much we own is another way to stunt meekness. When Paul said that the love of money was root to all kinds of evil he was taking his cues from Jesus. Jesus warned against the love of money (otherwise known as greed). Jesus, Paul and many saints throughout history have decried the accumulation of money and possessions because they knew how deadly they could be to our design. Jesus said, "Beware! Guard against every kind of greed. Life is not measured by how much you own" (Luke 12:15 NLT). He taught his disciples to pray for daily bread because he knew that humanity was designed to be dependent on God and satisfied with simplicity and sufficiency. Accumulating stuff is carbon monoxide to the soul. It puts to sleep our spirit and then poisons it. The meek have learned to be satisfied with daily bread. They realize that when we finally get the possession we crave, it is almost always followed by discontent. Learning to be content with little is a sign of meekness.

Still, wealth is not an automatic forfeiture of a meek spirit. Here too our pre-Fallen genetic memory reminds us that we were made to be in a place of abundance. Creation as we see it described in Genesis was opulent in its scale and intricacy. Abundance and meekness must not be mutually exclusive if God created such an extravagant environment for humans whom he imprinted with his own meek image.

Nonetheless, I believe the design of the man and the woman was not for conspicuous consumption, but for complete satisfaction with sufficiency. Gluttony makes us physically uncomfortable because our bodies were not made to

Nativity by Gary Nauman. Linocut.

overconsume. Our design becomes twisted when our desire for food (and nearly everything we perceive as enjoyable in the material universe) exceeds our ability to digest it, when we can't stop gorging ourselves even after our need has been met. This broken quest for more drives our lust to accumulate and stimulates pride as we consider how thoroughly we deserve such excess.

DOWNWARD MOBILITY

If ever there was a person who, during their lifetime, really did deserve to be rich, famous and powerful, it was Jesus Christ. Oddly enough, the one who legitimately could have lived in unspeakable wealth, commanded universal praise and wielded global power was on a downward mission. Jesus is a picture of perfect submission borne in meekness.

Jesus could have entered humanity as a fully competent, independent, highly skilled adult. Instead he chose to submit to the messiness of human birth at a time when child mortality was frighteningly high. He also chose to submit to poverty and obscurity, born to an unwed teenage peasant in an oppressed and forgotten corner of the Roman Empire, when it would have been natural, even obvious, for him to have been born into the household of an emperor.

In those days, if you predicted an eclipse accurately, you were welcomed into the courts of kings. As a young man, Jesus could have *ordered* an eclipse. He could have suspended gravity before the rulers of the world or done any number of mighty feats which would have proved his supremacy over creation. In so doing he would have gained the worship of global power brokers. Satan outright offered him all the kingdoms on earth, but Jesus refused. Instead, he became a simple carpenter and lived most of his life in obscurity, building simple dwellings, or maybe boats or furniture. Later he became a teacher not unlike the scads of other rabbis moving about with a brood of disciples. He was so ordinary, in fact, that when he returned to his hometown with the ability to teach and perform miracles, his neighbors, who just knew him as the carpenter's boy, were absolutely baffled.[2] Jesus chose a basic, blue-collar trade for most of his life and then pursued the life of a humble teacher for three years when he could have ruled nations.

I suppose Jesus could even have chosen a hostile takeover of the world. Alexander the Great, at Jesus' age, very nearly took the planet by military force a few hundred years earlier, and a handful of Vandals sacked Rome just a few hundred years later. Jesus surely could have conquered the planet with only a few thousand angels. He told Pilate he had access to twelve legions of angels. That's about sixty thousand. To possess such power and to allow people to publicly humiliate and kill him is a mystifying picture of descending status. The kingdoms of the world were his for the conquering; instead, he allowed himself to be conquered by a few weak, fallible men.

As Creator, Jesus possessed the ultimate form of power, and yet in meekness he submitted to the ultimate form of obedience. It would have been just and right for him to become global king; instead he became as one of the least of us humans and surrendered himself to a wrongful trial, conviction and execution. In taking this downward path, Jesus left us an example. After washing the disciples' feet, he said, "Since I, your Lord and Teacher, have washed your feet, you ought to wash each other's feet. I have given you an example to follow. Do as I have done to you. I tell you the truth, slaves are not greater than their master. Nor is the messenger more important than the one who sends the message. Now that you know these things, God will bless you for doing them" (John 13:14-17 NLT).

Just before being captured and abused, Jesus said to his disciples, "As the Father has sent me, so I send you" (John 20:21). Some have understood this to mean that Jesus sends his followers in the very way that the Father sent him—incarnationally—that they might become real to people who are lost and in trouble, which almost always means subordinating any desires and plans for ascendance. Maybe that's why Jesus ordered the disciples not to take any food or money or extra clothes when he sent them out on their training mission to proclaim the good news. He was teaching them the way of descent, the way of vulnerability and need. Maybe he was sending his disciples as the Father had sent him, a fragile, needy baby born into a family situation where he would have been considered the illegitimate child of a tradesman who married a pregnant girl. He did not endow the disciples with lordly status by outfitting them with fine clothes and mounting them on majestic steeds; rather, he ordered them to leave the little they had behind, sending them out penniless, homeless and on foot.

This idea of following Jesus on a downward journey—this bizarre call to divest yourself of this MONOPOLY™ world, give your resources to the poor and draw near to the One who gave up all he had so that he might draw near to us—has captured the imagination of saints in every age. St. Francis and Clare, Mother Teresa, and a handful of others are the famous ones, but most of those who have pursued downward mobility have lived in anonymity and will not be known to us on this side of history. That's a consequence of the downward journey; very few become widely known, and those who do, do so without trying. The downwardly mobile reject opportunities to "run with the horses" in order to crawl alongside the poor, lost and broken. They could live in mansions, but that's not where the sex-workers and street people hang out, so instead they live in shacks. Some have turned down illustrious careers to care for someone in need. Others have grown up in poverty and have chosen the challenge of a medical or law career in order to return to their neighborhoods to serve. These are the choices they make to follow Jesus on a path that puts them alongside people who will not be able to advance their status or their power or even repay them in any material way.

There are those, of course, whom Jesus calls into places of power and influence, but not for their own gain or comfort. God gives power to a few as a trust, a stewardship, to be used as a protection for the weak and to guard against the exploitation by the strong—not as a means to increase the power holder's own portion in the world. In Psalm 72 the psalmist describes such a leader:

Give the king your justice, O God. . . .
For he delivers the needy when they call,
    the poor and those who have no helper.
He has pity on the weak and the needy,
    and saves the lives of the needy.
From oppression and violence he redeems their life;
    and precious is their blood in his sight. (vv. 1, 12-14)

The powerful will be judged based on how they used their power. Did they leverage their money, fame or authority for their own selfish purposes or to advance the position of other powerful people, or did they use it for those who have no voice? "The LORD enters into judgment / with the elders and princes of his people," says the prophet Isaiah. "The spoil of the poor is in your houses. / What do you mean by crushing my people, / by grinding the face of the poor? says the Lord GOD of hosts" (Isaiah 3:14-15). The man or woman who uses God-given power for personal gain— whether for positional power, financial power, relational power or religious power—will answer to the One who loaned them that power in the first place. (In chapter six we'll deal with the question of how submission, obedience and meekness should look when those in power are corrupt.)

Jesus is the clearest example of someone who held more power than any person on earth has ever possessed yet did not use that power for personal gain. In fact most of the super-hero, divine-power-zing he could have flung around, he never touched. He lived in simplicity, he loved in extravagance, and he led in meekness. Instead of commanding lightning to strike as a show of force, he calmed storms. Instead of conjuring up decadent feasts for himself, he multiplied a simple meal of fish and bread to feed others. The first time his miraculous power showed up he transformed one hundred gallons of water into wine for a friend's wedding, and he did it in such a way that only servants knew the true source of the miracle. Jesus is the picture of the fusion of power and meekness.

"Take my yoke upon you, and learn of me; for I am meek and lowly in heart" (Matthew 11:29 KJV). Following Jesus on the downward journey does not mean you will never have power. It only means that you will never use it for yourself.

MODEL CHILDREN

As Jesus' ministry heated up, there was quite a bit of interest among the disciples about which one of them was greatest, so much so that an argument broke out. Of course, every time one claimed he possessed the most important position next to Jesus, it meant that the position of the others slipped down a notch (like when you're ten and have a friend who can smoke when all you can do is puff on rolled-up pepper). Each disciple wanted to be greater than all the others, and they sought some kind of metric with which to prove their supremacy.

Maybe they employed the kind of thinking that fuels leaders who are climbing toward greatness today: think big, turn your setbacks into comebacks, leverage your passions to build an empire, put yourself at the center of the action.[3] This is the kind of thinking that gets rewarded with status and power in this world, and there were likely some first-century versions of these sayings that military leaders or successful merchants employed to achieve dominance over their rivals. But personal mission statements or strategic planning or any number of things that can move companies and commanders from good to great didn't appear on Jesus' list of what will make you great in his kingdom. In fact, he turned the whole idea of the greatness pursuit on its head:

> Then they came to Capernaum; and when he was in the house he asked them, "What were you arguing about on the way?" But they were silent, for on the way they had argued with one another who was the greatest. He sat down, called the twelve, and said to them, "Whoever wants to be first must be last of all and servant of all." Then he took a little child and put it among them; and taking it in his arms, he said to them, "Whoever welcomes one such child in my name welcomes me, and whoever welcomes me welcomes not me but the one who sent me." (Mark 9:33-37)

The must-read list for every leader in Jesus' kingdom includes titles like *Be Last! Five Easy Steps to Becoming Everybody's Slave* and *101 Ways to Welcome Children.* There is a certain tongue-in-cheek humor with Jesus on this, a kind of irony which struck at the very heart of their desires for greatness. Jesus wasn't just showing them a better way of obtaining the thing they wanted; I believe he was attacking the very nature of their quest. He was saying, "Why all this jockeying for position? If there is a position worth jockeying for it's last place, because that's where I hang out. The attitude required to get down on your hands and knees and make a six-year-old feel welcome is what you should be striving after, not this ladder-climbing, puffed-up posture."

When Jesus placed that little child in the midst of the Twelve—a group including burly fishermen—in answer to their question about who is the greatest in the kingdom of heaven, the disparity must have been almost laughable: twelve grown men, seasoned by intense ministry experiences; apostles now in their own right having been sent out two-by-two to preach, heal and raise the dead; towering in stature over what might have been an eight-year-old little girl or boy. The physicality of placing the child "among them" was intentional. Jesus wanted them to appreciate the distance required for them to get from where they were— muscling for power and authority—to where they needed to be— vulnerable, dependent, meek and trusting. In fact, in another incident where the disciples were elbowing one another for first place (Matthew 18:1-4), Jesus went so far as to say that not only could the disciples not be great in God's kingdom unless they humbled themselves like a child, they couldn't even enter without the simplicity and humility of a child.

Rather than holding up political, religious or commercial leaders as pictures of greatness, Jesus encourages us to model ourselves after children. If that's not a call to downward mobility in a culture intoxicated with growing wealth, power or fame, I'm not sure what is.

In my church we have once or twice called the preteen children to the front of the church to pray for people during prayer ministry time. Usually when we do this we ask adults not to share their problems with the children because we want to respect appropriate boundaries; instead we ask adults simply to come and let a child pray for them. There is something powerfully simple about the faith of children, and it's reflected in their praying. A number of people in our church have been healed of physical and emotional problems through the prayers of our children. This could be very damaging to the ego of someone who wants to be known and celebrated for her extra ordinary abilities in healing prayer. When ten year olds achieve what has eluded many, it is time to ask, "What does a Jesus-loving child have that religious, sophisticated adults lack?" The answer is faith born of meekness and simplicity.

The disciples, however, didn't catch on right away to Jesus' meaning about becoming like kids; not long after one of their arguments, while eating the Last Supper, they fell into another argument over who was greatest. Matthew tells us it was provoked by a bold power-grab when James and John came to Jesus with their mother, begging for the two top posts in Jesus' administration. Jesus tried once more to convey just how different power in his kingdom looks in comparison to how we see power used in the world:

> The kings of the Gentiles lord it over them; and those in authority over them are called benefactors. But not so with you; rather the greatest among you must become like the youngest, and the leader like one who serves. For who is greater, the one who is at the table or the one who serves? Is it not the one at the table? But I am among you as one who serves. (Luke 22:25-27)

At this point, Jesus' ministry was in recession . . . at least by most any measure people today would use to gauge the success of a company or nation. Instead of going from good to great, his ministry was about to go from bad to worse. Perhaps if the disciples had known and comprehended what was ahead there wouldn't have been the tussle for power that was going on among them.

The way of the world, the way of most leadership manuals, the way of many large churches and ministries, even the way of Jesus' disciples was to seek greater status, authority, resources and recognition. But polarities in the kingdom of God are reversed. Up is down and down is up. Childlike meekness, invisible servanthood, seeking last place in a pecking order—these are the definitions of greatness in the coming kingdom. Such things spell death to pride.

PRACTICALLY MEEK

Rich Mullins, a Christian singer-songwriter who died in the 1990s, exemplified the celebration of meekness in exchange for the pursuit of wealth and status. Perhaps the struggles that my "Turtle" friend and others like him face in the pride-swelling limelight were instructive to Rich. He installed some safeguards to keep his ego in check and his meekness alive. For example, although he was making a lot of money before his death, he chose to live in a trailer across from a Navajo reservation on $24,000 a year. He told his accountant not to tell him how much money he had so that he could give it away more freely.

The people we turn into gods because of their acting or singing or athletic abilities, or even their great Christian ministries, usually suffer a crippling self-absorption that humans were not built to endure. Rich fought to keep it real and to be real to those on the margins. If we want to stay alive spiritually, we have to be near the spiritual Life-Giver, and he hangs out with the despised and rejected in places that require us to be ever journeying downward.

Rich was likely aware that climbing the Christian ministry ladder can be a deceptive cover for satisfying the ascendancy quest. That is why he worked to keep ego in check.

Having spent my entire working life in ministry, I am constantly tempted to build ego-fulfilling empires. In 2001 I worked very hard to follow the voice of Jesus in placing university students in slum communities of the developing world for the summer. My hope was that a few would hear Jesus' voice to take up residence among the poor as an act of worship and service. Since then the ministry has grown, and with it, the temptation for ascendancy. There is hopefully more than a shred of altruistic thirst for godly transformation of students and love for the poor in me, but if I'm honest, there's far too much pride, status, authority and power-mongering in me as well. How do I know? Because when I attempt to move downward, it hurts. When I give away large pieces of this ministry to younger, less experienced staff I feel the loss. When I turn down opportunities to speak in an attempt to injure my self-serving quest for Christian celebritydom and to guard time with my family, there is a sweet, painful dying inside.

In my years of ministry I have stabbed again and again at my genetic call to ascend, doing my best to accept God's invitation to die the death of a mustard seed. At times it has meant refusing raises. I've turned down the walled office with a window in favor of a cube set back a ways. If I get free first-class upgrades when I travel, I give them to those I travel with. These are my silly little attempts to become like a child, because I recognize my insatiable desire to look cool and grown up, imagining myself puffing away on some sort of successful ministry cigarette, blowing a long, easy stream of smoke out the side of my mouth while I squint my eyes and talk about how God has blessed my megaministry.

My wife, on the other hand, is one of the meekest people I know. When we needed more money to pay for my master's program she thought nothing of taking up a paper route. She's marked by an amazing ability to listen to others deeply and is often sought out by those who are lonely. And while she doesn't frequently get invited into positions of power, she is precisely the sort of person whom I believe is most capable of wielding it with deference to the powerless.

Henri Nouwen said, "The descending way is a way that is concealed in each person's heart. But because it is so seldom walked on, it is often overgrown with weeds. Slowly but surely we have to clear the weeds, open the way, and set out on it unafraid."[4] The times when I succumb to the call of pride—when I flash my headlights to let the jerk who cut me off in traffic know that I was in the right and he was in the wrong, or when I fixate on some great accomplishment I've achieved—are often followed shortly thereafter by an unexpected emptiness. There is a profound disappointment in desiring a large volume of blog traffic only to gain it, and then to watch that traffic trail off over time. Promotions are good for about a monthlong ego buzz and then the burden of the added responsibility sets in. But when I choose the downward path of a child, shaking off the grown-up expectation of sophistication and worldly success, I find a kind of giddy freedom. It's because the Architect made me to be meek. It was part of his blueprint and his intention for me to operate in such a way as to create the least drag on the flight of my soul.

THREE

SUBMISSION IN OUR LEADERSHIP-INFATUATED CULTURE

When I was in college I dropped acid . . . literally. During my sophomore year I worked on campus for a research laboratory. I cleaned the glassware that professors and grad students sullied with their experiments. Beakers, flasks, cylinders, funnels, pipettes and test tubes would be carted into my windowless room by the laundry basket–full and I would clean them. If you think it's hard getting dried cereal off of a bowl, just try dried beryllium sulfate. Beyond scrubbing the glassware with a soap mixture I had to submerge the items in an acid bath made of concentrated hydrochloric and concentrated nitric acid. From time to time I would need to clean the acid vat into which I dipped the glassware, and I was instructed by my supervisor to wear safety gear. I thought of his instruction more as advice than rigid policy. Besides, the glass cleaning room was my domain. I was in the best position to make my own decisions without some distant, out-of-touch rule-book-writer telling me what to do.

One hot day, when it was time to change the acid vat, I decided to obey the safety instructions as far as my gloves. As for the rest of my attire, I was wearing shorts, a short sleeve shirt and no goggles. As I was toting two bottles of concentrated hydrochloric acid over to the vat, the bottles slipped out of my hands. The tops were the first things to blow off as the bottles landed upright and shattered. The acid spewed up into my face like a geyser. I stood there dripping with concentrated hydrochloric acid and considered differently the instruction of my supervisor. Maybe it was more than advice. Maybe I should have done what he asked even if I thought it unnecessary and excessive. Maybe I should wash the acid off my face and think about this later.

I managed to keep my face mostly intact, though I had second and third degree burns everywhere the acid touched, even my eyelids. Disregarding the orders of my supervisor was a declaration of independence from my boss. If one of his commands was inconvenient, or if I disagreed, I could adjust the rules to suit my own understanding of the job. I paid the price for my insubordination for months afterward as my face healed.

Submission is a quality humans do not readily embrace. True, some cultures value it more highly than others, but generally speaking submission is a posture of defeat, and defeat is not valued in any culture that I'm aware of. The reason submission is avoided is because it almost always involves some kind of dying. If someone asks you to do something that you have no objection to doing, it's not really submission because it doesn't involve subjugating your will or plans to theirs; you're simply doing what's already agreeable to you. I can't very well order my children to go to an amusement park or eat dessert first and then boast about how well they submit to my authority. Submission is submission when doing what is asked of me grates against my will, my plans or my desires; it offends the almighty "I" and puts me under the rule of someone else. Submission requires me to die, and dying is never very pleasant. We might therefore be tempted to ask, since submission is so destructive to our independence and sense of self, can't we do without it altogether?

The problem is, if we want to be spiritual people aligned with God, our submission-resistant tendencies become a hindrance. This uncomfortable act of allowing our will to be subverted by another is necessary—even critical—for spiritual growth and peace with God. Indulging the natural tendency to do whatever we want enslaves us to our flesh, because the self-ruled person will never suffer the indignity of submitting to anyone, not even to God and his law. "The mind that is set on the flesh is hostile to God," Paul wrote. "It does not submit to God's law—indeed it cannot" (Romans 8:7).

Oddly enough, the first time the Greek word for submit, *hypotassō*, appears in the New Testament is when it's used about Jesus, who submitted to his parents. Apparently, even God willingly submitted to others—so it should not surprise us that he asks submission of us. Paul urged his readers to submit to governing authorities (Romans 13:1) and to submit to one another out of reverence for Christ (Ephesians 5:21). Likewise, Peter called followers of Jesus to "be subject to one another, and be clothed with humility: for God resisteth the proud and giveth grace to the humble" (1 Peter 5:5 KJV). Whether slave or master, husband or wife, young or old, parent or child, at some time or another everybody in the Bible is adjured to submit to someone: "submit yourselves therefore to God. . . . Humble yourselves before the Lord, and he will exalt you" (James 4:7, 10).

Submission appears to be a basic characteristic of the spiritual man or woman.

STAYING BEHIND IN BEDFORD FALLS
TO RUN THE BUILDING AND LOAN COMPANY

There is something magnificently transformative in the death that comes through submission which can be obtained in no other way, but those of us in the American church, in particular, embrace that death so infrequently that we've been crippled in our ability to live the life of humility required for spiritual vitality. I remember as a young manager of short-term mission programs for InterVarsity Christian Fellowship making plans to lead a group of students to Israel/Palestine in order to work with Palestinian refugees. Since leading trips was part of my job description, and since I hadn't led a project for a few years, I felt it was important to lead another team. So I communicated my plans to Dan, my boss at the time, and began working with an organization in Bethlehem to receive us.

What was particularly energizing about preparing to lead this project was the fact that I had for years dreamed of relocating long-term to a challenging part of the world in order to make a difference. Janine and I had applied to a couple of mission agencies not very long before this proposed short-term trip, but for a variety of reasons the application process had derailed. I was beginning to feel as though I were suffocating in middle-class normality, swallowed up by mediocrity. Instead of living in the Middle East, we owned a home in the Midwest. We spoke only in English, shopped at malls, were planning to have our second child and in the near future would own a minivan. It all felt so average. All of my holy ambitions to pour myself out sacrificially in desperate parts of the world had evaporated. Now, in planning this project, I could sense the life beginning to creep back into my drooping spirit. The thorny issues surrounding Israelis and Palestinians inspired me to dream big and fed my excitement for breaking down the short-term-mission tourist mentality by taking students into difficult places and demanding a lot from them before, during and after the trip. This trip had all the makings of something that would jumpstart my flagging sense of kingdom usefulness and push students to think critically about this fragile and war-torn part of the planet.

Just weeks before going to Bethlehem to set up the project, Dan called me into his office. Somehow my communication to him about leading this trip had not been clear, so he was surprised that I was thinking of personally leading this team. Who would be around to help with any emergencies that might arise while I was away? he wanted to know.

This reasoning seemed flawed to me. The other mission groups I had been sending all over the world operated just fine without me being on call, and I told him so. I was the one who knew firsthand what was required to support the teams who were on the field. At that time there were only about a dozen projects each year anyway, and it was rare for a team to need my assistance while they were out of the U.S. Besides, there were others in the office who could help in case of an emergency. Dan, however, was immovable on the point. Under no circumstances did he want me out of the country while other teams were abroad.

I was mad and disappointed. I felt like George Bailey in the movie *It's a Wonderful Life* being asked once again to stay behind in Bedford Falls to run the building and loan company while others were allowed to pursue their dreams overseas. In fact, I so thoroughly disagreed that I considered whether I should quit my job and seek employment elsewhere, some place where I was trusted and could make decisions without being treated like a child.

In the end, I submitted to Dan. I undid my plans to lead a team to Israel/Palestine and stayed back that summer to babysit the phone. As I had predicted, there were no emergencies that others could not have handled. But I'm convinced today that obeying Dan was the absolute right thing to do. Submission to him was critical to building a strong trust relationship and growing my character. In fact, I can now see that dying to my own plans in order to obey a boss with whom I disagreed was one of the most important things I've done in my career. Laying down my plans dealt a much-needed blow to my messianic aspirations and my pride.[1] Submission to Dan was more transformative than any conference or book has ever been for me because to do it, I had to die to myself, and learning to die to myself has come in handy. The needs and requests of my wife, kids, colleagues and bosses have made death by submission a spiritual-growth pathway for me.

There are, of course, times when my thoughts and opinions prevail over others. Submission is best offered only after some sort of healthy discussion and disagreement. But at those times when, for a variety of reasons, it's right to lay down my opinion and submit, a sweet dying and growing can occur.

BORN DICTATORS

If we were made to be in submission—if that's the path of true spirituality—then why are we born dictators? Perhaps this is the original sin passed down: that rebellion from God's generous boundaries for us in our attempt to become our own god. Whatever the reason, from the moment we take our first mouthful of air we seem to instinctively know how to make our will known and demand that others submit to it.

By three months old our eldest daughter, Hannah, could get her new parents to do just about anything she wanted through the power of her bloodcurdling cry. We tried every parenting trick in the book to get her to agree with our notions of sleeping, eating and a generally civilized schedule, but we quickly discovered that submission ran against the grain of her genetic code, just as we discovered it did for her brother and sister. Our children intuitively resisted any form of control.

If this inherent desire to be subject to no one and master of everyone is allowed to persist, it's called being spoiled. And if this tyranny continues into adulthood, it's called being childish, which is quite distinct from the "becoming like a child" that Jesus encouraged. Not only does such a person become impossible to live with, they also become eternally discontent with life, because even if they can manipulate everyone around them there are simply too many circumstances outside their control to satiate the desire of their ever-hungry selfish will.

Self-centeredness cannot be permitted to live on in the healthy, spiritual adult. The opposite of submission is rebellion, and although rebellion is generally considered cool in American culture it doesn't seem to be considered "cool" by God. Even the most well-intentioned "rebel" who is committed to justice is bound to be wrong sometimes and will hurt themselves and others if they never submit to anyone. There is simply no way around the fact that we need to come under others.

As Americans, freedom and independence are pathological obsessions. Our natural tendency to resist authority has been put on steroids. "Live free or die!" is the philosophical foundation for our country and stands in stark contrast to the philosophy of the kingdom of God, which tells us to die in order that we might live free. We Americans are cowboys who believe submission is for yellow-bellied, lily-livered, chicken-hearted cowards who don't have the guts to fight for what they believe is right.

The problem with such independent, anti-authoritarian, self-righteous breeding is that it has no place in the upside-down kingdom of love, selflessness, submission and service ushered in by Jesus. The most beautiful picture of submission is submission that's offered freely, not submission that's demanded under threat.

While true submission means subjugating your will to another's, it's still voluntary subjugation. Jesus' Sermon on the Mount gives us a picture of what this looks like:

> Do not resist an evil person. If someone strikes you on the right cheek, turn to him the other also. And if someone wants to sue you and take your tunic, let him have your cloak as well. If someone forces you to go one mile, go with him two miles. Give to the one who asks you, and do not turn away from the one who wants to borrow from you. (Matthew 5:39-42 NIV)

This willing submission is not very consistent with my American ideology. Sermons like this prove that Jesus' teachings were un-American. He consistently called his followers to a lifestyle of dying well: laying down the things they craved, like a place at his right hand, and picking up things they abhorred, like crosses. But this call was a call to offer our submission to others, not to let others take it. In the above passage, the one offering submission is the one in control, willingly taking extra steps to prove that their submission is not being coerced but is freely given.

LEADERSHIP SCHMEADERSHIP

The word *servanthood* bears the scourge of the red, squiggly underline in my version of Microsoft Word, which betrays the fact that *servanthood* is a nonword. Those who write our dictionaries and program our computers want to split the word up: "servant hood." What could that possibly mean anyway, a servant's hood? Or a hood that's a servant, or even a neighborhood made up of people who serve? These, apparently, are more legitimate concepts; no red underline. Put the two words together, however, and we have a problem. *Motherhood, brotherhood, manhood, likelihood, knighthood,* even *babyhood* don't get flagged as misspelled. But *servanthood* has no place in the English language, nor does it have much of a place in American culture. And I fear that even within the church the idea of quiet, humble submission and service has been usurped by the value of exercising authority over others.

Why are we so infatuated with leadership? Why is following so disagreeable to us? Try this experiment. Go to Amazon.com and do an advanced search within Amazon's book listings. First, search for books that have the word *leader* in the title. My search today shows me that there are over 29,000 results. Number one on the list is a book about exerting the kind of leadership that will transform the life of your dog. Apparently becoming the alpha-leader over your pet is a high felt-need.

Now do another advanced search, this time with the word *follower* in the title. I found a little over 1,000 results. Of those one-thousand-plus titles, however, some are leadership books that happen to have the word *follower* in the title, like *From Followers to Leaders*. Others are marketing books, like *The Power of Cult Branding: How 9 Magnetic Brands Turned Customers into Loyal Followers (and Yours Can, Too!)*. Thankfully there are a growing number of books examining the benefits of following, even though some of them, of course, are published by places like the Center for Public Leadership and most of them are marketed to organizational leaders.

The word *follower* does bring up a great number of titles referencing the people who follow Jesus, so you would think that submission and following are qualities Christians might be experts at and therefore might write and teach about, showing how we as humans need to live out the value of submission. But a similar title search at Christianbook.com brings up an even higher ratio of leader to follower books. I also found that Christian leadership is the subject of more "leadership institutes" in a Google search than any category besides civics and business. Next to people running the government or businesses, Christians appear to be among those most concerned about the practice of leading, not following.

Now search a Bible database to see how many times the word *lead* is used in the Gospels.[2] In the NIV *lead* occurs twenty-one times, and most of the references are negative: Judas leading the crowds to apprehend Jesus, the blind leading the blind, the road that leads to destruction and so on. None of them are commands to the disciples. Jesus never instructs his disciples to "become the leaders you were meant to be." In fact, religious leaders in the Gospels were often threatened by Jesus' upside-down kingdom that's destined to be inherited by the meek. With just a handful of exceptions, those who had religious or political leadership roles in the first four books of the New Testament were antagonists to the gospel.

Jesus wasn't nearly as obsessed with leadership as American Christians seem to be. In fact, looking at the Gospels, quite the opposite is true. There are eighty-six references to the word *follow*—four times as many references as there are for *lead*—and most of the uses of *follow* are positive, many of them direct commands. "Follow me," for example, was a phrase Jesus used twenty times in the Gospels. Jesus was far and away more concerned about his disciples' ability to follow well than he was about their ability to lead well.

Submission is implicit in the command to follow. When Jesus said, "If any want to become my followers, let them deny themselves and take up their cross and follow me" (Matthew 16:24), he was telling us that following him and denying self are inseparable acts. "For those who want to save their life will lose it," he said, "and those who lose their life for my sake will find it" (Matthew 16:25). Submission, following, self-denial and losing your life . . . these were central themes for Jesus, yet I'm inundated with invitations to Christian leadership conferences designed to "stretch my leadership bandwidth." I don't think I've ever heard about a Christian conference focused on the practice of submission.

Make no mistake: Jesus was convinced that his followers would be light in dark places and salt in a world of gruel—the leaven of society, elevating people, systems and structures around them. And if influence is a form of leadership, then Jesus certainly intended for us to lead. But the poor in spirit, the mourners, the meek, the hungry, the merciful, the pure, the peacemakers and the persecuted are the people Jesus said were blessed (Matthew 5:1-12). I suppose there are some leadership books and conferences that hold some of these qualities up for leaders to embrace. Still, the people paraded before us as leaders whom we're to emulate are usually successful business or ministry professionals. Very few are invisible, obscure, simple followers.

GREAT ONES

A group of us once invited a homeless man to be the keynote speaker for a conference. His name was Glenn, and he had some of the qualities of the people Jesus called "blessed" in the Sermon on the Mount. For fifteen years he had lived on the streets of the Tenderloin district in San Francisco and, just two months prior to the conference, had gotten his life stabilized with the help of Jesus and a few of his followers. He was as nervous as all get-out to speak in front of two hundred college students from universities like UC—Berkeley. But this humble, grateful and seriously weathered man was a wonderful example of those whom Jesus called great. The ways Jesus described what it means to be great are often radically different from the traits that mark the Fortune 500 leaders or megaministry leaders who are invited to speak at conferences. Great ones by Jesus' reckoning were the pesky children who climbed on him, an obscure, bug-eating prophet who railed against prominent leaders, and slaves who washed dung from

Glenn

people's feet. These were the profiles Jesus used to give us a picture of what great ones are like.

You'd think, then, that I would be able to find a dozen Christian books on dung-cleaning submission for every one book on exercising authority over others. But books on submission simply don't sell in America. In this leadership-besotted climate, can you imagine trying to market a book titled *Extraordinary Submission: Turning Your Company's Strongest Leaders into Subservient Followers?* The only way you could hope to break even on such a title is for a few business moguls to claim that it was "a must-read for every leader."

One of the most recognized contrasts to our leadership-infatuated culture is Mother Teresa, who displayed character qualities which should be normative in the kingdom of God. Yet even she has been co-opted by the world's leadership gurus in an attempt to master the leadership craft for personal profit.[3] Jesus himself has been dissected by Christian and non-Christian leadership scientists alike in order to unlock the keys of leading so that we can "bigger" things like profits, market share or seats in a pew, though I daresay that filling a building for an hour on Sunday was not a chief concern of Christ.[4] Politics and capitalism are the chief headwaters of leadership philosophy and practice. Too often the qualities of their "great ones" become the qualities that define greatness for the followers of Jesus. But the things that work in a system designed to leverage power for financial gain or political dominance don't necessarily work in a system where gaining the world may forfeit your soul. It's not possible for the church to drink from those streams and remain uninfected by the power dynamics floating in them; the "politics" of the kingdom have more to do with meekness, submission and dying to self than they do with exercising authority to increase my share in this life.

Brad Jersak, teacher at Fresh Wind Christian Fellowship in Abbotsford, British Columbia, describes in his book *Kissing the Leper* how their church fellowship has been led by some of their developmentally disabled members. A number of them have an uncanny ability to stand up and blurt out just the right Scripture at just the right time. They are humble, simple, Spirit-filled and occasionally socially inappropriate men and women, and they so clearly fit Jesus' description of those who are great in the kingdom of God that the church has ordained a couple of them as pastors. These are the kingdom profiles of greatness that need to be lifted up before us to help us get beyond our overly sophisticated definitions of leadership and success. If the kingdom to come will be inherited by the meek, where the poor and marginalized are given seats of honor at the head table of the wedding banquet; then let us learn to submit . . . to God and to one another, even if that means sitting at the feet of the homeless and developmentally disabled instead of the wealthy and the intellectual. Because until we learn to die to the definitions of success in this world, we cannot know what it really means to live successfully in the kingdom of God.

PRACTICALLY LOVING

Marriage has provided me great opportunities to advance in the art of submission and dying. Don't get me wrong; it's not that I don't like being married, it's just that I prefer having my way all the time. If I could be married *and* always do what I wanted, life would be ideal. But marriage, and any other real form of community living, forces us to concede that there are other sentient life forms in the universe besides us.

Having kids was another nail in the coffin of my independence-loving self-absorption, carrying me way beyond the sainthood of watching a romantic comedy instead of an action movie. Having kids means cleaning up poop and vomit. It means sleep deprivation at near insanity levels, peanut butter in the DVD drive, teenage angst erupting in your face unprovoked and unbelievably high car insurance. These sacrifices are a form of submission powered by love.

"Submit to one another out of reverence for Christ" (Ephesians 5:21 NIV), Paul urges. Romantic love is one picture of mutual submission. One of the greatest portraits of romantic love appears in the movie *Titanic.* I'm not talking about Jack and Rose, the principal characters; I'm talking about the elderly Mr. and Mrs. Strauss. When it came time to load passengers into the precious few lifeboats in the real-life drama of the Titanic's demise, Ida Strauss refused to board without her husband. After more than forty years of marriage she insisted, "We lived together so we will die together." The two of them surrendered their spots on the lifeboat to their servant, Ellen Bird. The movie version portrays the elderly couple lying down together on their bunk to die, comforting each other as water rushes in to overtake them.

But as beautiful as forty-year married love might be, it's normal for two humans to feel that deeply about someone who loves them back. It takes no supernatural power to love a person who loves you, and romantic love generally can't last very long if it's not returned. Likewise, healthy friendships also have a component of mutual affection and submission. Our friends love us, which is partly what motivates our love for them. Loving our family may take a little more effort than loving a spouse or friend, since we don't choose our family, but even this doesn't require special virtue. In fact, if you want to see exceptional examples of familial love and submission, look no further than the Mafia. So, while subjugating my will out of love to my wife, kids, family and friends is a beautiful picture of submission, it's nothing truly extraordinary. As Jesus said, if you love those who love you back, what credit is that to you?

To love those who don't love you back, however, is radically countercultural. Loving and submitting to those we don't like is hard for us to wrap our minds around, and even harder to accomplish.. In the book *Life of Pi,* the story's Hindu protagonist is baffled by Christ's demonstration of this kind of love by his willingness to submit to death on the cross.

> That a god should put up with adversity, I could understand.
> . . . But humiliation? Death? I couldn't imagine Lord Krishna
> consenting to be stripped naked, whipped, mocked,
> dragged through the streets and, to top it off, crucified—and
> at the hands of mere humans, to boot. . . . Why not leave
> death to the mortals? Why make dirty what is beautiful, spoil
> what is perfect? Love. That was Father Martin's answer.[5]

To love others in a way that transcends romance or friendship or family; to love people who can give nothing back and who have little in common with you; to love people with radically different backgrounds or worldviews; to love people who have treated you badly; to esteem them above yourself just because you choose to, just because it's within you to do so—that kind of love requires divine energy, because it involves a deeper level of submission and dying.

The love of Christ is expressed in nearly every passage of the

Gospel narratives. Touching the leprous and confronting religious authorities are snapshots of his power to love, giving us clues as to how we're to love. But John records one particular incident as the defining act of Christ's love before his crucifixion. It's a picture of the deep love and submission that only those empowered by God can experience.

It was just before the Passover Feast. Jesus knew that the time had come for him to leave this world and go to the Father. Having loved his own who were in the world, he now showed them the full extent of his love.

The evening meal was being served, and the devil had already prompted Judas Iscariot, son of Simon, to betray Jesus. Jesus knew that the Father had put all things under his power, and that he had come from God and was returning to God; so he got up from the meal, took off his outer clothing, and wrapped a towel around his waist. After that, he poured water into a basin and began to wash his disciples' feet, drying them with the towel that was wrapped around him. (John 13:1-5 NIV)

John makes a point of telling his readers that Jesus was acutely aware at this moment of his supremacy over all creation. He knew that he had authority over Caesar, over the emperor of China, over every human being, every demonic creature, every angel and death itself. With this knowledge in the forefront of his mind, he decided to wash the feet of his helpers. It was a filthy job that required him to remove his outer garment, and at least one disciple, Peter, was unable to bear the uncomfortable irony of the Son of God washing the dung and dirt from what was considered one of the most profane parts of the human body. It was a slave's work, not the work of a Lord and Master.

As the disciples sat in shock and bewilderment, Jesus got dressed, sat down and asked, "Do you understand what I have

Washing the Disciples' Feet by Gary Nauman. Linocut.

done for you?" John records no reply on the part of the disciples—I imagine them sitting silent and confused—so Jesus finally answered his own question: "I've set for you an example, that you should do as I have done for you." The one we are to mimic literally washed the crap off of dirty feet knowing that hours later one pair of those freshly cleaned feet would lead an angry mob to capture, try, humiliate and crucify him. This act of submissive, practical love is the pattern with which we're to craft our relationships.

I have on a few occasions found myself gripped with this love. My stepfather was a great man who was good at giving focused attention to me, asking questions about the little details of my life, and showing genuine interest in who I was and what I did. But he was an alcoholic, eventually dying of the disease, and in his later years he became emotionally abusive to my mother in ways that made me angry. The last time I saw him alive was when I came home for my brother's funeral (who also died of alcoholism). There were periods of time where I could barely muster the power to speak with my stepfather by then. But as I left him on this occasion, I chose to embrace him, and I clung to him long after it's socially acceptable for two men to hug. As we stood there in that hold of affection, I whispered a prayer of blessing into his ear. To hug my stepfather was an act of submission, and I discovered that there was divine love available to me in that moment if I would allow it to take hold of my heart, if I could find the strength to submit to the love impulse nearly hidden, covered as it was by my desire for revenge. When I allowed love to subvert revenge, it was surprisingly easy to embrace my stepdad with genuine affection— the kind of dung-washing, submissive love that Jesus calls us to give to those who wrongfully treat us.

In his book *The Irresistible Revolution* Shane Claiborne quotes seminary professor Will O'Brien: "When we truly discover love, Capitalism will not be possible and Communism will not be necessary."[6] God's love confounds the self-interest required for capitalism to function and renders moot the control essential for Communism. Who would attempt to make large profits from selling something to their spouse or child, and why would you need to force equality through coercion and control if you were convinced that people would act out of genuine love? While the gift of leadership is a particular gift to a few, it is expected that any of us claiming to be a disciple of Jesus would be appropriating this sort of selfless love in near-offensive proportions to all, especially to those who are in a state of profound unlovability to us. To do as Jesus has done for us will require us to regularly dethrone our desire for selfishness and control and allow true submission to one another to take root.

Leading is easier and more enjoyable for me than following, because following always requires me to die. Harboring a righteous indignation toward someone who has wronged me takes no special effort. But love puts to death revenge. This kind of love is not easy. It is exceedingly hard to die to a posture of judgment when you're in the right. Loving the wrongful or irritating person and submitting to those with whom we disagree is an exercise in dying.

But for me the real test of submission and dying usually involves money. Jesus said where your treasure is there your heart will be also. I've discovered that my heart and my money are painfully bound together, and my attitude about money and possessions reveals something about my spirituality and my readiness to submit to God and the ways of his upside-down kingdom. Relinquishing wealth can become a doorway to experiencing the sort of death that brings real life and intimacy with the Creator. This is the topic to which we turn in the next chapter.

REPENTANCE AND
THE DEATH OF
PERSONAL WEALTH

ot long ago I had a dream that I was in Mexico
relaxing on a bench after having eaten a meal. I watched as a
clean-shaven, neatly dressed Mexican man and his daughter
approached me. I knew, as you can only know in a dream, that this
man and his daughter were believers. I also knew that they were
beggars despite their well-groomed appearance.

When the man came up to me I saw that he cradled a booklet in his
arm. The title of the booklet was *Evangelical*. He turned to me and said
only one thing: "I have no food."

This presented a dilemma. I had given all my change as a tip for the
meal I had just eaten. I only had a ten-dollar bill left. I could either give
him everything or nothing. There wasn't anything in between. I
considered going somewhere to break the ten, but I knew that I needed
to respond in the moment.

"I'm sorry," I said. "I just ate at a restaurant and have given all my change for a tip."

The man and his daughter simply walked away without saying anything and I woke up.

The state of our soul is uncomfortably bound up with our generosity. In Matthew 25, Jesus distinguishes those who enter eternal life from those who enter eternal punishment based on their generosity toward people in need. Generosity to "the least" is like generosity toward Christ, and tightfistedness to "the least" is like tightfistedness toward Christ. When we're in a state of submission, we relinquish the notion of personal ownership. We're no longer independent but instead become dependent. Therefore we're not free to use the Master's resources solely on ourselves. We must first consider the One to whom we're submitted.

Paul once wrote to the Corinthian church about a collection they were taking up for the believers in Jerusalem who were suffering under tremendous material need: "For your generosity to them and to all believers will prove that you are obedient to the Good News of Christ" (2 Corinthians 9:13 NLT). The Corinthian generosity to the poor in Jerusalem was evidence of their obedience to the gospel. We get our term "evangelical" from the Greek word *euangelion,* which means, "good news"; most often it shows up as the word *gospel.* As Paul's words to the Corinthians indicate, submission and obedience to the gospel are not evidenced by our words or theology as much as by our actions— including the use of money.

The man in my dream holding on to the book titled *Evangelical* was really holding on to the good news. The very first time that *euangelion* is mentioned in the New Testament is Matthew 4:23: "Jesus went throughout Galilee, teaching in their synagogues and proclaiming the *good news* of the kingdom and curing every disease and every sickness among the people" (emphasis mine).

So, though the word "evangelical" *(euangelion)* has come to carry certain political, cultural and social freight, today, it really refers to a kingdom, a realm, a government, more than a mental assent to a doctrine or words that are spoken or a prayer that is prayed. This *euangelion*-good-news-kingdom was a dominion. A place where penitent prostitutes were welcomed, self-righteous Pharisees were locked out and people who were broken got put back together. It was a place easily found and entered by little children and those like them, but nearly impossible for the rich and self-sufficient to enter. This dawning government defied the notions of religiosity in Jesus' day. He told the most respected religious authorities of his time, "Truly I tell you, the tax collectors and the prostitutes are going into the kingdom of God ahead of you" (Matthew 21:31).

A key characteristic of this kingdom is that it has an economy, or at least there are economic implications to being a resident in the kingdom. When news of this kingdom is announced in the Gospels, for instance, financial consequences often follow. In the Sermon on the Mount—one of the first times the kingdom of God is mentioned in Luke—Jesus reveals the constitution of the kingdom, declaring, "Blessed are you who are poor, / for yours is the kingdom of God" (Luke 6:20). Apparently this kingdom belongs in a special way to those who are poor, and while this probably includes people who have a variety of kinds of poverty (poverty of body, possessions or spirit) it most definitely includes the materially poor. In fact, those who have been cut out of ownership in the kingdom of MONOPOLY™ find that they are the chief owners in the *euangelion* kingdom.

Flipping through the channels on TV one Sunday I came across a televised preacher. Part of his message was that God intends for Christians to be wealthy. The preacher urged everyone to take out their wallets, hold them up, place a hand over the top and proclaim, "You will be full, full, full!"

It is true that God created humanity to flourish and to be in an environment of abundance. The word *shalom* in Hebrew carries the sense of prosperity. Conveniently, many have taken this to mean that they themselves should be personally wealthy, having many resources that they alone control, despite the poverty of those around them. If God himself was poor when he took on flesh, it is difficult to understand how someone who says they follow such a servant Savior could think that accumulating wealth so that you can be financially independent is at all biblical. Financial independence from our Creator is an illusion, and cordoning off money so that it is not connected to the rest of humanity and creation is unsustainable should everyone get the same notion.

So if submission to God and obedience to the gospel of the kingdom is measured at least in part by my generosity to those in need, and if the kingdom which Jesus ushered in belongs to the poor and will be inherited by the meek, then how can I be allowed or even encouraged by church leaders to pursue financial gain for the purpose of accumulation or lavishing wealth on myself? Why is the great body of church leadership and governance literature coming from the capitalistic-minded, for-profit, MONOPOLY™-game world which rewards self-oriented unmeekness? Can a kingdom destined for the meek and destined to be great news to poor people really run on principles which drive wages down and prices up in order to maximize profit, and which make celebrities out of CEOs?

I received my bachelor's degree in business administration, and the main source of energy fueling the marketing and management philosophies I studied was the quest for "biggering." Biggering your company and biggering your market share and biggering your profits. A company that grew from ten employees to one hundred was better than a company that shrunk from one hundred down to ten. We were taught that successful businesses were motivated by the desire to capture a market and drive competitors so far into the dust that they had to fold. This was moving from good to great in the business world. Companies that did this were to be studied and emulated.

In *Blueprint to a Billion*, author David Thomson identifies the "7 essentials to achieve exponential growth." In studying the companies that exhibited exponential growth in their climb to a billion dollars in revenue, he found some common traits, the rocket fuel that can propel companies into the kind of biggering that anybody in business would love to see. For example, if your value over other companies is not clear, you should seek to become what Thomson describes as a "Category Killer." Category Killers are companies like Home Depot which will "optimize a market by attacking the existing incumbents with a better-faster-cheaper value offer."[1] This kind of company espouses a predatory mindset.

I suppose there's nothing inherently wrong with selling a shovel for less, or selling it in such a way that it's deemed more valuable than the same shovel at the mom-and-pop hardware store next door, but the drive-someone-else-into-bankruptcy-in-order-to-achieve-exponential-revenue-growth mentality is clearly not a mentality that fits in the kingdom of God.

A CENTRIFUGAL ECONOMY

When God set up his economic principles on earth around 1500 B.C. in the form of ancient Israel's land-ownership and money-lending laws, I don't think he had *Blueprint to a Billion* in mind. For example, if one family was able to buy up the land of another family due to business prowess or the other family's business misfortune, the successful family had to deed the land back to the unlucky family less than fifty years later.[2] The gentility, the meekness, the love inherent in this law flies directly in the face of

MONOPOLY™. As does another instruction from Leviticus 25: "When you make an agreement with your neighbor to buy or sell property, you must not take advantage of each other" (v. 14 NLT). Even more radical, when an ancient Israelite's crops or business failed so badly that they were forced to borrow money from a lender, that lender was commanded to forgive the loan if the borrower couldn't pay it back within seven years.[3] God's economic principles laid out in the Old Testament law actively worked against predatory practices. They didn't allow for the exponential biggering of revenue. What they did do was protect the little software producer from getting swallowed by the ancient Israeli version of Microsoft.

The motivation for multiplying wealth is also absent from the kingdom economics present in the New Testament, though I suppose you could say there is a sort of "biggering" theme in some of Jesus' teachings on the kingdom. He likens God's dawning government to a mustard seed or a little bit of leaven which is nearly invisible until it dies, at which point some kind of metamorphosis takes place and big stuff starts to happen. A massive pile of dense, tasteless flour-mud is transformed into light, tasty bread, and a dirt-covered speck breaks out of the ground and becomes an enormous plant that produces a potent spice (Matthew 13:31-33). The point to Jesus' teaching on the impact of the kingdom, however, seems to be less akin to a little church becoming a big church or a little ministry becoming a big one, which is where much of the MONOPOLY™-inspired Christian-leadership teaching takes us. It's more akin to a little church that changes a city or a little ministry that changes the world. You might even say it's about a small thing whose death produces widespread transformation. What appears to be an insignificant crumb swallowed up by the sludge around it is really a powerful ingredient that absolutely revolutionizes everything that

The World's Smallest Seed by Jim Janknegt. Oil on canvas.

touches it. In Jesus' parable, the mustard seed doesn't grow, it dies, and the speck of leaven doesn't become a giant ball, it dissolves. Too often the leadership culture has suggested that Jesus was more interested in bigger-ness than he was in the transforming power of little things that die sacrificially. One could even argue that the leavening power of the kingdom works against the accumulation principles that drive capitalism, principles that concentrate wealth and power into the hands of a few. In fact, bread made with 50 percent leaven will have freakish results, and planting too many mustard seeds in too little dirt will produce nothing. The very quality of the leaven and the mustard seed requires that they be grossly outnumbered by the flour-mud and dirt which bury them.

At one point in his travels (Luke 19:1-10) Jesus invited himself over to the house of a rich scoundrel named Zacchaeus who had acquired his wealth by gouging others with "off the record" taxes which he pocketed. The religious people were appalled that Jesus would choose such corrupt company, but Zacchaeus was so thrilled that Jesus chose to simply hang out with him that he gave half of his possessions to the poor and repaid what he cheated people times a factor of four. Flinging his wealth out like that triggered Jesus' response, "Today salvation has come to this house." He knew that this man understood the economics of entering God's kingdom. By contrast, a young ruler with a lot of money rushed up to Jesus to ask him how to inherit eternal life. After assuring Jesus that he had kept the commandments since his youth, Jesus said he lacked one thing: "Go, sell what you own, and give the money to the poor, and you will have treasure in heaven; then come, follow me" (Mark 10:21). The man went away grieving because of his many possessions. Jesus then said, "How hard it will be for those who have wealth to enter the kingdom of God." Jesus knew that the forces of the kingdom that worked against personal accumulation would turn many wealthy away, causing them to grieve that they could not overcome their addiction to possessions.

The economic forces of the kingdom of God appear to disperse wealth more than concentrate it. Those who are living under the good-news-to-the-poor kingdom laws of love and meekness find that money does not bunch together but, rather, spreads out.

Nothing reveals our view of material possessions quite like divvying up a deceased relative's wealth. It's a little like when, as kids, my siblings and I were forced to divide the last bit of dessert. Everybody's eyes seemed to measure the cake differently, and my piece was never as big as the others'. It baffles me how a sliver of food can spawn so vehement an argument, even if you're not hungry. Dividing inheritance wealth is like that, only magnified. Splitting even small sums of money can generate disputes that rend families to pieces for years. It was just such a dispute that prompted Jesus' sermon on the centrifugal quality of kingdom economics.

A man in the crowd called out, asking Jesus to force his brother to divide their father's estate with him. Jesus refused to get into the middle of the row and instead told a story. It was about a landowner who must have had a blueprint to a billion, because his field was so fertile that it produced more wheat than the man could eat, more even than he could sell, and what was left over after eating and selling was too massive to store in his existing barns. So the rich man's solution to this exponential growth was to "bigger" his storage capacity. That way, he reasoned, he would be able to say to his soul, "You have ample goods laid up for many years; relax, eat, drink, be merry." This sounds very much like the unquestioned philosophy of retiring rich that motivates so many of us to accumulate personal wealth. But the retirement plan that God advises is different. Jesus called this man a fool because he was going to die on the very night that he decided to store up the wealth he had amassed for some future, ill-defined party. Instead of eating, drinking and being merry, his money would likely just stir up a bitter inheritance war (Luke 12:13-33).

Providing for a time when you will not be able to work or saving a modest amount to give to your children is not the thing Jesus is decrying in his parable. The punch line to the story is this: "So it is with those who store up treasures for themselves but are not rich toward God." Amassing wealth for oneself and being rich toward

God are mutually exclusive forces. It's as if richness toward God is measured by the amount you give away to others in the present, as compared to the amount you store up for yourself for the future. It is the "I better hang on to my money just in case" mindset that inspires my tightfisted reluctance to give a ten-dollar bill to a poor man and his daughter who need it now. The economy of the kingdom is an economy of dispersion, not an economy of accumulation, and our lack of submission to the King of this kingdom is reflected in how much money we hoard.

From this story Jesus launched into a sermon on the crippling fear of not having enough that motivates our hoarding tendencies. Building personal wealth dominates the economic thinking of our world, because independence and self-sufficiency are highly prized, and being in a position of dependence upon God or anyone else is actively avoided. But to be meek is to recognize your dependence. Jesus wasn't issuing a warning against storing up treasures to those fretting about having enough for another car or being able to pay the cable TV bill at the end of the month. He was talking to people who worried about whether their food would last until the next harvest, or whether their sandals and tunic could keep them reasonably covered one more year. He charged them to let go of their faithless anxieties about whether they'd have enough to eat or wear: "Therefore I tell you, do not worry about your life, what you will eat, or about your body, what you will wear. For life is more than food, and the body more than clothing" (Luke 12:22-23).

Jesus reminded his followers that God is not stingy when he provides for the earth—birds and flowers—because these are things he made and that he possesses deep affection and concern for. How much more, then, is he motivated to provide for the well-being of people, the crown of his creation, the only things in the universe made in his image? This human pursuit to satisfy the cravings of the body should not dominate kingdom people. "For it is the nations of the world that strive after all these things," Jesus said. "Instead, strive for [God's] kingdom, and these things will be given to you as well" (Luke 12:30-31). The apostle Matthew recorded it this way, "But strive first for the kingdom of God and his righteousness" (Matthew 6:33). More than being motivated by our own empire, or even striving after our basic needs, we are to strive after the establishment of God's kingdom and the righteousness and justice which rules it.

So what does richness toward God and striving after his kingdom look like? Jesus gave the answer in the grand finale statement of the passage: "Sell your possessions and give to those in need. This will store up treasure for you in heaven! And the purses of heaven never get old or develop holes. Your treasure will be safe; no thief can steal it and no moth can destroy it. Wherever your treasure is, there the desires of your heart will also be" (Luke 12:33-34 NLT).

Those who are meek and who are submitted to the government of God will seek for his kingdom to come before all else, because they treasure this kingdom more than they treasure personal wealth. They are attentive to those who are weak and who are trampled underfoot by the powerful. They turn into great centrifuges of wealth, spinning their possessions out to those in need and stretching their arms out to those on the margins of society. Without violence they work to see power that has been used to reward a few powerful property owners converted so that those in distress are attended to.

This isn't trickle-down economics where a few at the top might slop some of what they have accumulated over the edge so that a drop or two trickles down to the masses at the bottom. Kingdom economics is pictured in the poor widow who was so insanely generous that she gave away the little she had to live on (Mark

12:41-44). In kingdom economics the followers of Jesus pool their resources and then dole them out to each one as they have need (Acts 4:32-34). Widows and orphans are cared for in their distress (James 1:27). Homes are open for the homeless and clothing is given away to those who need it (Matthew 25:35-36). The economic blueprint in God's kingdom works against personal increase and selfish accumulation and works toward distribution out to the extremities. Perhaps that's why Jesus said that it was impossible to serve both God and money; people can't submit to the desire for personal accumulation *and* submit to the desire for God at the same time. That may also be why Paul said that the love of money is at the root of all kinds of evil (1 Timothy 6:10). And why John wrote that you couldn't have the love of God inside you if you had enough but didn't respond compassionately to a brother or sister in need (1 John 3:17).

This is why word of this coming kingdom is such great news for the poor; the *euangelion* of the kingdom is tied to a dispersion of wealth. This means, though, that those owning the greatest share in the MONOPOLY™ economics need to repent at this kingdom's coming—and repentance, incidentally, is one of those qualities that awakens meekness.

REPENTONOMICS

I am a big-picture sort of guy, which is another way of saying that I am terrible with details. This is especially apparent when following maps or driving directions. On long trips it is not unusual that in the process of going from one highway or interstate to the next I get turned around. Sometimes, well into the trip, I will notice I am getting closer to the wrong end of the state. Repentance is not just apologizing (especially if there are others in the car or people waiting for me at the other end) while I continue to careen down the same highway in the same direction. No matter how sorry I am to be going the wrong direction, it is not repentance until I find a way off the highway, and then find a way to get back on going the opposite direction. There are a number of places in the Bible where that repentant turning around is tied to money.

When John the Baptist preached, people came out in droves to confess their sins and be baptized by him. It was a spiritual bath, a ceremonial cleansing accompanied by a profession of sorrow over sin. But John verbally attacked the penitents who came out to be baptized, accusing them of being self-serving snakes, slithering out of the grass as if fleeing an approaching brush fire: "You brood of snakes! Who warned you to flee God's coming wrath? Prove by the way you live that you have repented of your sins and turned to God" (Luke 3:7-8 NLT).

From John's perspective, repentance produced fruit, proof that they had exited the highway and turned around, proof that they were operating out of humility and meekness rather than pride and self-sufficiency. The fruit didn't consist simply of confession and baptism; there was something more practical by which to measure humble sorrow for sin. So the crowds asked him what they should do. What would give evidence that they had really humbled themselves and repented? To each group that asked John this question, he gave an economic response.

The crowds asked, "What should we do?"

John replied, "If you have two shirts, give one to the poor. If you have food, share it with those who are hungry."

Even corrupt tax collectors came to be baptized and asked, "Teacher, what should we do?"

He replied, "Collect no more taxes than the government requires."

"What should we do?" asked some soldiers.

John replied, "Don't extort money or make false accusations. And be content with your pay." (Luke 3:10-14 NLT)

Repentance was not genuine if you hoarded clothes or ignored the cries of the hungry. If you were a tax collector, you hadn't truly repented if you continued the common practice of adding a surcharge to people's tax in order to line your pocket. Soldiers were notoriously underpaid, but they couldn't repent and continue to force people to give them money at the point of a spear. What's more, they had to find contentment with their meager income. These are the things that would serve as sure signs that the people coming to confess their sins were serious about repentance. The proof is in the pudding—or in this case in the padding of their wallets.

This kind of practical repentance requires subjugating the fear and greed that inspire our hoarding, and releasing the things that feel desperately precious to us: our possessions and our money. Repentance is proved by actions which are meek—setting aside selfish accumulation and insuring the needs of others are met. What we do with material wealth is an outward and visible sign of an inward reality.

The connection between material generosity and repentance shows up later in Luke as well. In chapter 16 Jesus tells a story about two men: a rich man who feasts sumptuously every day and lives in a palace, and a diseased beggar named Lazarus who sits outside the rich man's gate longing for some trickle-down economics or a blueprint to a billion. The rich man dies and goes to a place of torment. But when impoverished Lazarus dies, he is carried away by angels to a place of peace near the great patriarch, Abraham. We are not told whether Lazarus or the rich man possessed faith or unbelief to merit their very different fates (the rich man's reference to Abraham as his father is a reference any good Jew of Jesus' day would have made, and is not enough to bring him into a place of rest[4]). All we know is that, while alive, the rich man allowed Lazarus to remain in a state of desperation while in eyeshot of his mansion. This state of living a life of excess while watching the poor rot seems to bear some relationship to the rich man's tormented destiny because it is a window into his lack of humility and repentance. Throughout the Bible this selfish tightfistedness is a picture of the unrepentant heart.

In eternity the roles are reversed and now the rich man is the beggar: "I beg you to send [Lazarus] to my father's house—for I have five brothers—that he may warn them, so that they will not also come into this place of torment" (Luke 16:27-28). The rich man's focus had been on personal accumulation to the exclusion of the poor. In those days as today, great wealth was locked up in the hands of families. The rich man knows that in his father's house, among his male siblings (wealth passed only to the males), the same self-absorbed blueprint to personal wealth which had landed him in trouble also exists in the hearts of his brothers. He reasons that "if someone goes to them from the dead, they will *repent*" (Luke 16:30, emphasis mine).

Abraham tells the rich man that his brothers have access to the words of Moses and the prophets, which are sufficient for them to realize their need for wealth-dispersing repentance. After all, Moses instituted the law that solemnly warned Israel not to withhold money from a needy neighbor as the rich man had done to Lazarus, lest the poor neighbor "cry to the Lord against you, and you . . . incur guilt" (Deuteronomy 15:9). And Isaiah the prophet brought word of God's judgment to the leaders of Israel for filling their houses "with things stolen from the poor" and for "grinding the faces of the poor into the dust" (Isaiah 3:14-15 NLT). There was enough information in the Scriptures for the rich man's brothers to realize that stockpiling wealth to the exclusion of the poor was a picture of their unrepentant hearts and therefore a sign of their ultimate destiny.

Again and again, the law and the prophets testify to the economic implications of submitting to Yahweh. Scripture is clear that the fruit of knowing him and believing that he is good can be measured by openhandedness toward those in need, intolerance toward oppression, a welcoming spirit toward the wandering alien and readiness to obey him even at great personal cost. These are the outward signs that indicate an inward turning and a posture of meekness. Maybe this is why Jesus tells the parable of the sheep and the goats in Matthew 25. The sheep, like Lazarus, are welcomed into the fullness of the kingdom for all eternity. The goats, like the rich man, go away to eternal punishment. The criterion for determining who goes where is how they treated "the least."[5] Treatment of the marginalized is the truest picture of what's in our hearts. Kingdom dwellers visit prisoners, feed the hungry, and take care of the sick and the stranger. Those who get cast out of the presence of the Lord cling to their lives and their resources, leaving the needy in their condition.

In the book of Revelation Jesus brings a warning to the church in the city of Laodicea, telling them that he is about to spit them out of his mouth because of their financially self-sufficient attitude: "For you say, 'I am rich, I have prospered, and I need nothing'" (Revelation 3:17). This is a New Testament church, mind you, a body of believers who lived no more than a handful of years after Jesus' resurrection. Some of their leaders may have even known him while he walked the earth. These people had the apostle John as their bishop for goodness sake—the guy whom Jesus entrusted his mother to. Nonetheless they had become rich enough as a body to be self-reliant, and self-reliance poisons meekness. Their one-time profession of humble faith and dependence on Jesus had been eroded by their prosperity. Jesus' call to them in their state of financial independence is a word for many rich churches today: "Be earnest, therefore, and *repent*" (Revelation 3:19, emphasis mine).

The fruit of Laodicean repentance, just like the fruit of repentance today, will result in centrifugal economics. The call for wealth-dispersing, oppression-breaking, poverty-lifting repentance is laid out by the apostle James to the scattered body of Christ:

> Come now, you rich people, weep and wail for the miseries that are coming to you. Your riches have rotted, and your clothes are moth-eaten. Your gold and silver have rusted, and their rust will be evidence against you, and it will eat your flesh like fire. You have laid up treasure for the last days. Listen! The wages of the laborers who mowed your fields, which you kept back by fraud, cry out, and the cries of the harvesters have reached the ears of the Lord of hosts. You have lived on the earth in luxury and in pleasure; you have fattened your hearts in a day of slaughter. You have condemned and murdered the righteous one, who does not resist you. (James 5:1-6)

PRACTICALLY REPENTANT

I want to live a penitent life in all meekness. But proof of my repentance has been slow in coming. While my dream about being in Mexico was just that—only a dream—I know myself well enough to know the truth. I do not fully depend on God for my daily bread, and that produces a tendency to be stingy. Jesus knew that the source of tightfistedness was either greed or fear, attitudes which run in direct contradiction to kingdom economics and betray our lack of true faith and meekness.

In my dream I wish I had opened my wallet and said to the man, "Hey, look at that. I've got ten bucks here and I really don't need it. You have it." To do that, though, requires me to die to a personal-wealth orientation, and this death is the beginning of true repentance. My unreadiness to die to self-reliance, my conviction that I must seize control of my destiny by hoarding cash, reveals a nagging insecurity about who I really trust and prevents me from abandoning myself fully to God's care. Financially carefree kingdom people are generous—not because they have big barns full of money, but because they know that God feeds the birds and is perfectly capable of providing for them.

En route to the Marquette University financial aid office to plead for more money for our daughter, Hannah, Janine and I passed a homeless man with a cardboard sign that said, "Out of work. Need help. God bless you." Janine looked at me. "Do you have some cash?" I opened my wallet. There were a few ones and a ten. I gave Janine a one. "How about that ten?" she asked, motioning to my open billfold. I winced and pulled it out. *Stab! Take that you money-grubbing, unrepentant nature.* Once again God was speaking to me and inviting me to die to self-reliance and become meekly dependent on him. It wasn't a mortal blow, but Janine and I at least winded the greedy creature living in me. One of these days I hope to be living a repentant, "evangelical" lifestyle. When I do, the Lazaruses living outside my gate will be the first to experience it.

FOLLOWING AND THE DEATH OF COMPARISON

The dissatisfaction that comes via comparison is the chief engine that drives materialism and consumerism. It plays to our ascendancy quest and our twisted desire for more than we need. The computer you bought last year that was the most amazing piece of technology in the world is now an embarrassment to its inventor and looks like a crude, technological piece of flint used by a primitive and uneducated Cro-Magnon geek when compared to the technolicious shiny thing that just came on the market. Following Jesus can, early on, feel exciting and radical . . . right up through the first costly sacrifice or the invitation to follow him onto a path that others are not taking.

There are times when I look at friends, even other Christians, and start to doubt the path of meekness, submission and obedience I'm on. It's as if obedience is made impotent through the act of comparison because comparison gives me real-life examples to point to in order to justify why I shouldn't follow Jesus into the way he's calling me to walk.

The "come follow me" invitation Christ has issued to me has been in the area of mobilizing others. I'm most alive when I'm launching people into mission. I've found, though, that as I've followed Jesus on this path of igniting and inspiring people to go to the desperate and lonely places, especially into the slum communities of the developing world, my biggest challenges come when I stop to compare myself with others.

One day, a leader of an agency that works among the poor and that had been receiving a steady stream of college students from the "launch pad" I'd created wrote to ask a question—and his question played directly to the temptation to compare myself and doubt my commitment to follow Jesus as a mobilizer. He wanted to know what real experience I had had living and serving in developing-world slums. What were the credentials that gave me authority to address kingdom work in slums? The answer was simple enough: none. I had never done anything but short-term work in slum communities and tons of reading. I had never accomplished the "real" work, the hard work of slogging out an existence in a slum community while raising a family, loving intractably poor neighbors and watching the kingdom come in sustainable, long-term ways. The implication of that little question for staying on track with my calling was huge.

What on earth am I doing? I asked myself. *Have I really heard God correctly? What kind of hypocrite calls men and women to move into the world's worst poverty from the comfort of an American, middle-class lifestyle?*[1] "God," I prayed, "wouldn't it just be easier to use someone in this role of mobilization who had lived the life I'm calling others into? Why not ask someone more qualified to call others to give their lives to the desperately poor?" I was, in a sense, saying "no" to following, having disqualified myself from Jesus' call by what seemed to me to be pretty reasonable criteria. I simply did not have the credentials nor had I earned the right to call people into this kind of mission.

I'm sure that's what Moses must have been thinking when God called him to lead the liberation of his people in the exodus. Moses had the benefit of hearing God directly (though we're not given details on how he heard) at the burning bush, calling him to lead a slave race of Israelites out of Egypt. Moses replied by asking, "Who am I that I should go to Pharaoh, and bring the Israelites out of Egypt?" (Exodus 3:11). Then Moses posed one disqualifier after another: "But who should I tell them sent me? What if they don't believe me? You know I never can't speak no good!" God patiently knocked down one objection after another as quickly as Moses propped them up. Finally, in exasperation Moses pleaded, "O my Lord, please send someone else" (Exodus 4:13).

I love and serve the poor around me, and I lead people for weeks at a time into slum communities. But Janine and I simply do not sense that we have God's call or permission to relocate to a slum permanently. I was already insecure and embarrassed to call people into a mission that I wasn't called into. This question asked by a leader who worked in a mission devoted to placing people among the poor tempted me to set aside my calling. I don't know if my temptation to quit brought about the same results as Moses' plea—kindling "the anger of the LORD"—but I did hear God speak into my desire to abandon the journey based on my lack of qualification. I sensed him saying, "Of course you're not qualified. But it's my prerogative to call the unqualified to whatever mission I choose. Don't ponder whether you're qualified; ponder whether you will obey."

INCOMPARABLE JESUS

If Jesus had compared himself to any earthly ruler he might have disqualified himself. Caesar and Herod had radically different life experiences and training than Jesus did. Creating and ruling a kingdom were things that they were bred to accomplish. They were raised in households that leveraged everything toward the end result of raising a ruler. I seriously doubt Mary or Joseph knew how to prepare a king.

Looking at the privileges men like Herod and Caesar enjoyed could have also undermined Jesus' entire calling and destiny. Even though women followed Jesus, he never experienced the joy and romance and challenge of a wife like the other rulers. Marriage was ordained at creation—leaving your father and mother, cleaving to your spouse and uniting in sexual union—and has been enjoyed by earthly kings. But Christ never experienced it. "Oh, Father," Jesus might have said, "If Herod can take his brother's wife, surely I can show people what a good monogamous relationship looks like? You know all things. You know the loneliness of this itinerant life. Moses, David, Solomon—they all had wives. All things are possible with you, so can't I still accomplish what you want of me with a wife?"

Prophets, priests and political rulers in Israel almost always enjoyed this aspect of humanity. It would have been easy for Jesus to justify marriage as he looked around at others. But it is apparent that God affords some the privilege of accepting a life of singleness for various purposes (for example, see Matthew 19:12). There's something about Jesus' affection for the church, his bride, which kept him on a path that didn't allow him to experience earthly marriage. Comparison in this area could have derailed him from his calling.

Comparison in the area of property ownership, too, could have distracted Jesus from his Father's plan. So far as we know, Jesus never owned a home. He was called to a life of wandering. Looking at Caesar's life as a standard could have prompted Jesus to ask his Father, "Dad, I'm needful of a home base. I fully intend to share it with others. I'm not asking for a fraction of what Caesar has, just a little place by the sea with an upper room for guests. With such a place I would build a training center and the first-ever Christian leadership institute." Jesus could have even used Scripture to justify the rooted life of a home and family. When Israel was in exile God commanded them to "build houses and live in them; plant gardens and eat what they produce. Take wives and have sons and daughters; take wives for your sons, and give your daughters in marriage, that they may bear sons and daughters; multiply there, and do not decrease" (Jeremiah 29:5-6). Verses like this could have given Jesus scriptural backing for buying a house in Roman-occupied Israel. But Jesus chose the discomfort of being a guest in others' homes or, at times, not even having a place to sleep (Matthew 8:20).

Jesus denied himself many good things and undertook many hard things. Comparison with Herod, Caesar, priests, prophets or even his ancestor David would have given Jesus justification for doing or avoiding just about anything. But Jesus wasn't going where anyone else had gone before. He didn't come to build the kingdom others had built in the past. If he compared himself with them, he could only hope to accomplish what they had accomplished. Only by incomparable submission could Jesus march headlong into a place of abandonment and crucifixion—something God had asked of no one else.

The same is true for you and me. The paths Jesus asks us to follow are often not the paths he asks others to follow. You can justify the avoidance of any task simply by finding the right saint and saying, "They never had to do this, therefore I don't either" or "I'm not as qualified as they were, therefore you must not be asking me to do this." You can also indulge any privilege you want by looking at other noble, godly people and saying, "They got to do these cool things and have all this wonderful stuff." But we are unique individuals, and God calls us to a long obedience in unique directions.

PETER VERSUS JOHN

If I had to guess which two disciples were the closest friends I'd have to say Peter and John. They were fishing buddies. In fact, they were in business together with three others: John's dad, Zebedee; John's brother, James; and Peter's brother, Andrew. But the four boys left Zebedee to take care of the fishing business by himself while they followed a rabbi from Nazareth. I'm not sure what happened with Andrew in this foursome, but Peter and the Zebedee boys, James and John, ended up becoming really close to one another and to Jesus—closer than any of the others. There were a number of occasions, though, where only Peter and John worked together. For example, Jesus sent the two of them out to prepare the Passover meal for everyone (Luke 22:8). Aspects of their friendship can be seen during the Last Supper, when Jesus told the disciples that one of them was going to betray him. Peter motioned to John, who was leaning his head against Jesus, and whispered something like "Ask him who he's talking about" (John 13:24). And after the resurrection Peter and John created a stir by healing a beggar as they walked together to the temple to pray (Acts 3:1). They also did time together in jail (Acts 4:3), which has a tendency to either enhance or destroy friendship. Later, the two of them set out together on a mission to Samaria (Acts 8:14).

So having likely grown up together, having hammered out a joint business, decided together to follow a rabbi and then been crushed side-by-side in the crucible of ministry, I bet that the two of them became extremely close. And I can't help but wonder if there wasn't a bit of competition between them from time to time.

Peter by nature seemed competitive. He was regularly going one step beyond John and the others, whether it was walking on water when no one else would dare consider it or vowing to die with Jesus when Jesus announced his death while the others stood around like lunks. We also see his competitive side when Peter and John raced to the tomb the morning Jesus was resurrected. John technically beat Peter to the tomb, but Peter defiled himself first by rushing inside the tomb, beating John to the empty grave clothes. Peter and John lived, loved, fought and served together. And on occasion they compared themselves to one another. Or at least Peter did.

We've already looked at the time John (along with his brother James) tried to outmaneuver Peter into the two positions of authority at Jesus' right and left hand in the coming kingdom. That had to hurt, to have your closest friends and partners in business and in ministry shove you aside in order to lock in positions that would leave you one notch below. But the clearest moment that Peter is tempted not to follow Jesus by comparing himself comes in chapter 21 of the Gospel of John.

In this passage, the boys are fishing on that same body of water where they had grown up and fished together before, the Sea of Galilee. And just like the day Peter accepted the call to follow Jesus, they had once again fished all night without catching a thing. A man on the shore called out to them to let down their nets on the other side of the boat. Ridiculous as it sounded after hours and hours of fishing right around that very spot, something compelled them to try it. Instantly an impossible haul of fish filled their nets. I picture them looking at one another with that "What the . . . huh?" look in their eyes. Then someone, probably John, had a flashback to that day a few years before when Jesus did the same thing, commanding them to lower their nets and subsequently filling those nets with a ginormous catch of fish.

John squinted to look at the man on the shore and burst out, "It's the Lord!" Peter, of course, jumped overboard to beat the others to the shore.

After preparing and serving his disciples breakfast (meal prep was usually the job of the lowest-ranking person), Jesus took a walk with Peter to talk about love. Jesus reminded Peter that he was not called to be a fisherman but to be a shepherd. Perhaps he sensed in Peter an abandonment of the call he had given him to follow, as Peter had denied him three times and now seemed to have returned to fishing for a living. We're not told why Jesus pressed Peter with the call to "feed my lambs" and "tend my sheep." It was somehow tied to the word *love*, which became central to their discussion. I suspect Jesus was telling Peter that to love him was to follow him, even into that place of kingdom service which did not seem obvious. Being a good Christian fisherman made sense to Peter. He was qualified for this. But Jesus was calling Peter into a ministry that didn't seem like a natural fit for him: feeding and caring for Jesus' flock. Peter's personality seemed better suited to the hunter/fisher role than the shepherd/nurturer role.

Near the end of this exchange, Jesus described the ultimate price of true love: martyrdom. Following Jesus as an obedient shepherd to the point of death disturbed Peter, however. Not because Peter was unwilling to love unto death, but because he knew that the fate for his closest friend—John—was different. Jesus told Peter he would be tied up and led where he didn't want to go: into martyrdom. John, on the other hand, was called to "remain until I come," which must have sounded a far sight better.

Peter turned and saw the disciple whom Jesus loved following them; he was the one who had reclined next to Jesus at the supper and had said, "Lord, who is it that is going to betray you?" When Peter saw him, he said to

Jesus, "Lord, what about him?" Jesus said to him, "If it is my will that he remain until I come, what is that to you? Follow me!" (John 21:20-22)

Comparison with his friend (and sometimes rival) motivated Peter to demand of Jesus, "Lord, what about him? Why is my fate different than John's? Why do I get tied up and led to where I don't want to go and he gets to remain until you come?" Peter was ultimately inferring this: "Jesus, I know how to divvy things up fairly so that both John and I serve you with equal cost. After all, he's the better nurturer, always talking about love and stuff. Why don't you just let me decide how to dish out our callings and their costs? Let me determine who feeds lambs and then gets tied up and led around where they don't want to go, and who gets to remain until you come." Perhaps there was even jealousy that John regularly identified himself as "the disciple whom Jesus loved."[2]

Following Jesus into a costly calling which is already a poor fit with our natural gifts and wiring will never be easily embraced if we look off to the side at those "other disciples" who seem to be more naturally gifted for the task, especially when our calling appears more costly than the calling of those who are better suited to the job. It starts to look as if Jesus loves them more. That kind of comparison derails humble submission and following.

INCOMPARABLE OBEDIENCE

John David and Heidi are friends of mine who several years ago followed Jesus into a slum in the Middle East. They lived on the second floor of a concrete box in a neighborhood of three million slum dwellers. In the summer, temperatures hovered around one hundred degrees in their living space, and in winter they could see their breath inside some mornings. Sickness and insomnia were among their closest companions—all because they were called by Jesus to "tend my sheep" among the poorest of the

John David and Heidi

Muslim poor, not as distant, remote-control church planters, but as friends and neighbors.

The kind of calling John David and Heidi are pursuing requires extremely limited contact with those who openly associate with the Christian community or with other expatriates. They don't believe that dietary laws, cultural identity, even the way one worships should stand in the way of a Muslim deciding to follow Jesus, and they are convinced that there is space within Islam to accept Jesus' death and resurrection and follow him as Lord . . . as Jesus-loving Muslims, however, not as those who consider themselves churchgoing Christians.[3] Such a calling and lifestyle is incredibly unique and has produced a cross of loneliness upon which John David and Heidi are ready to die. They're considered odd by their neighbors, looked upon as fools by other Westerners living in their city, and believed to be heretics by some of their Christian brothers and sisters, especially Middle Eastern Christians who think of Muslims as the oppressors.

Justin and Anne are good friends of John David and Heidi, and live not too far from my family in a mixed-income community here in Madison, Wisconsin. It's a spacious neighborhood made up of a cluster of condominiums which share a large courtyard and an area dedicated to fruitful garden plots. The people living in these condos with Justin and Anne all embrace common values such as environmental stewardship and community living. Justin and Anne are called to love their neighbors extravagantly in the hope that some will decide that Jesus must be the real deal. Even though Justin and Anne share with John David and Heidi a love for and calling to the poor as well as a commitment to simplicity, their lifestyles are radically different. Both have been tempted to doubt their paths, and comparison to each other only makes it worse.

Justin and Anne have faced a certain amount of false guilt: "Shouldn't we just sell it all and go live among the poorest of the poor like John David and Heidi?" Likewise, there are times when John David and Heidi are tested: "Jesus is obviously working

Justin, Anne and their boys

through godly Americans who love and serve him in nice neighborhoods. Surely we could live out our calling in a place of greater physical comfort and safety." But it is Jesus' license to call John David and Heidi to live in a poor Muslim slum and Justin and Anne to live in a New-Age, semi-Buddhist community in the United States. Each faces their own version of hardship, failure and ostracism. Each enjoys different kinds of joy, triumph and affection with their neighbors. Neither of these couples could adequately submit to Jesus' call if they looked to the other as the ministry "gold standard." In meekness and humility they must follow Jesus as best they know how.

PRACTICALLY FOLLOWING

Following Jesus implies that you hear his call. This can be more art than science. He is spirit, and more or less invisible, which can make communication with earthbound people like us a challenge.

I came home from work one evening to find a note from Janine. All it said was, "Hi dear. We're having spaghetti for dinner tonight. XOXO, Janine." I thought to myself, *That's nice. Janine is preparing my appetite for dinner.* Then I began to open the mail. After about twenty minutes I noticed that it was getting on to nearly 6:00 p.m. It was then that the note began to look different to me. What if she was not telling me what we were having for dinner, but in fact asking me to make dinner? Should I start supper? What if she wants a specific recipe? What if she really wants to make it herself because she has a special love of making spaghetti? Cooking comes more naturally to her than to me, and our daily patterns at present mean she does most of the cooking. But slowly and tentatively I began making spaghetti. As noodles began to boil, I vaguely recalled a discussion the night before about her running some errands and being home late. I felt a little better. Maybe I was on the right track.

I know Janine better than any other human being on earth. She is "flesh of my flesh and bone of my bone." I have lived with her longer than I lived with my parents or my siblings. In this instance, I happened to guess right. Dinner was ready just as she and the kids arrived back from an errand. I sat down to eat with my family, grateful that, despite my apprehension, I acted, rather than choosing passivity until I was absolutely certain.

If the most intimate human relationship possible—marriage—is fraught with weekly miscommunication (miscommunication only once a week either means we've had a great week of communication or I've been traveling and we've not had as much chance to talk), how is it that we expect the voice of God to always be clear and unmistakable before we act? This is the God who loves parables and stories and mystery, the God of whom it's said that his foolishness is wiser than human wisdom (1 Corinthians 1:25). His thoughts are not our thoughts.

We must live in the tension of hearing God's voice about calling and service without always having complete clarity on his particular will for us in a particular matter. Some kind of action is almost always implied in his love notes, even when it only appears to us to be an FYI. One of his notes shows up again and again, and goes something like this: "Dear ones: My kingdom is coming near and we're having a big party. The poor and marginalized are my honored guests. Evil won't be tolerated any more and justice will roll down like a river. The meek will be in charge. It'll be great. XOXO, Dad."

I used to think, as I pondered this recurring love note in Scripture, *Oh, that's nice. God is going to bring his government to earth some day and he's giving special preference to the outcasts and the meek.* But as time goes on and I don't see his kingdom dawning among the poor, the note begins to look different. What if God wants me to do something? What if this note is really an invitation to follow him, using all I have to bring this kingdom reality into existence today? What if in addition to caring for the poor around me, I am to use my gifts as a launcher to catapult others into the world's darkest, loneliest, most kingdomless neighborhoods?

The thing that kills my action on this one is not so much the sometimes-cryptic nature of God's communication, but looking at what others are or aren't doing. Not only must I deal with the challenge of understanding the parabolic (some might even say obtuse) ways God communicates with a guy who can't even understand his closest friend and wife, but I am also hamstrung by insecurities that are inflamed whenever I consider others' actions in comparison to mine. When I stop measuring myself against others and move forward even when God's word feels uncertain, it's easier to obey and to follow on a downward path into meekness and service. Only then can I step into the attitude and posture of a slave without regard for how it might appear to others.

SIX

SLAVERY AND THE DEATH OF ENTITLEMENT

On December 10, 1936, King Edward VIII became the only British monarch to voluntarily relinquish his crown. He didn't surrender the throne because he wasn't qualified to govern Great Britain, nor did he bail out of his royal right because of military or political pressure from an opposing foreign power. He gave up the title of king in order to marry the woman he'd fallen in love with, Wallis Simpson. Because she was considered tainted by divorce, Edward was faced with either reigning as king apart from her or marrying his love and renouncing his royal position to preserve the perceived integrity of the monarchy. People all over the world huddled around radios to listen to the crackly

King Edward VIII

pronouncement given by the king: "I have found it impossible to carry the heavy burden of responsibility and to discharge my duties as king as I would wish to do, without the help and support of the woman I love." Women swooned and men shook their heads at this uncommon display of self-deprecating love.

This event struck a romantic chord for so many people because it is the story of a man who possessed the highest form of power that earth can offer and turned it all down for the simple privilege of waking up day after day next to the woman he loved, a woman stained by her past. Most of the fairy-tale love stories are the other way around, much like the marriage of Prince Charles and Diana, where the royal marriage results in the commoner becoming a princess. The idea of a king abdicating his throne in order to marry a woman considered by many to be morally blemished was scandalously romantic.

The love of Jesus is more like the love of King Edward VIII than it is like the classic fairy tale—except that King Edward lived quite nicely as Prince Edward, duke of Windsor, for the rest of his life. He never had to experience peasantry or blue-collar labor, nor did he endure the humiliation of extreme servitude in order to be united to his love. Jesus' story, on the other hand, is the story of a great king who fell in love with a woman who, though of noble birth, ran away and prostituted herself to every man she could find. She so utterly ruined her reputation that no man would have her even as a secret lover. Her only recourse for survival was to sell herself as a slave for food and shelter. This high king, in order to simply draw near to her, not only left his royal position but also sold himself into the lowest form of slavery right next to her. He labored in complete meekness and obedience to those who were rightfully his subjects, eventually giving his life in exchange for her freedom. Now that's a love story.

Love has greater subjugating power than any dictator can

command because love dethrones self. The very definition of love is to put self second. Love inspires us to set aside our rights and privileges—our sense of entitlement—in order to serve another. Maybe that's why love is listed as the first and greatest commandment—"You shall love the LORD your God" (Deuteronomy 6:5)—and why love so thoroughly permeates the life and teachings of Christ. Song of Solomon says that "love is strong as death" (8:6), probably hearkening readers to the stories of lovers who give their lives for their beloved.

The love-struck will, without a second thought, shed anything that creates a barrier to the object of their affection, even if it requires severe acts of selfless service. This is what Jesus has done for us, and if we can get our brains around his sacrificial love, it may just inspire love in us, enabling us to do what he did: set aside rights in order to serve others. Understanding his love will feed our ability to love and serve even the least deserving person, and it will starve our sense of entitlement even when we possess great wealth, status or authority.

PAUL'S FASCINATION WITH THE SLAVE METAPHOR

Paul (known as Saul when we first meet him in the book of Acts) was a snob. He had a Jewish pedigree that was unquestionable (Philippians 3:4-6). He was schooled under the leading Jewish rabbi of his time, Gamaliel (Acts 22:3), who is believed to have founded the last of the great Pharisaical schools.[1] What's more, Paul was a Roman citizen in a day when there were at least as many people who could claim the title of slave in Rome as could say they were legal citizens.

Paul was a spiritual, academic and political elitist—and he despised a little sect of followers that believed a working-class Galilean was Messiah. This carpenter-rabbi's chief followers were reeking fishermen for goodness' sake, not to mention the rabble he gathered around him. The fact that he had women disciples, sitting at his feet and being taught by him, was scandalous enough (Luke 10:39). But that he would allow prostitutes to travel with him and his disciples put him completely out of respectable rabbi territory.[2] In some Middle Eastern cultures even today, having men and women traveling and learning side by side in a religious community is extremely questionable. Then there were the tax collectors; they were a whole other category of status-plummeting, Mafia-like figures for a rabbi to keep company with.

Probably the thing that would have most upset Paul, though, was the thing that ultimately got Jesus killed: his callous disregard for Jewish law and his irreverent comments about sacred things like the sabbath and the temple. Jesus was a heretic to Paul, and the fact that uneducated Jews were falling prey to his erroneous teachings meant that this cult had to be stopped at all costs. But on the Damascus road, on his way to round up a few more Christian heretics, Paul was blinded by love and became himself one of the heretical followers he had so strenuously denounced.

Paul went from holding a position of high status and rare privilege to being a despised slave of Christ and the church. So much so that at various times in his career, he was whipped, beaten, chased and imprisoned by those who hated Christ-followers. Once he was even stoned and left for dead. He had to endure hunger, thirst and lack of adequate clothing and housing, not to mention his constant burden of caring for churches—some of whom thought of him as a sniveling weakling.[3] Paul was a willing love-slave of Jesus, and as such was considered "the rubbish of the world, the dregs of all things" (1 Cor 4:13). His pedigree, his education, even his esteemed Roman citizenship took a back seat to the fact that he was first and foremost a slave of Christ. In fact, Paul used slave language quite a bit.

The words *doulos* (slave) or *diakonos* (waiter, servant or one who performs menial chores) show up in every single letter attributed to Paul in the New Testament as pictures of what it means to follow Jesus.

> Paul, a servant [literally "slave," (doulos) but often sanitized to read "servant"] of Jesus Christ, called to be an apostle, set apart for the gospel of God. (Romans 1:1)

> This letter is from Paul, a slave of God and an apostle of Jesus Christ. (Titus 1:1 NLT)

> The Good News has been preached all over the world, and I, Paul, have been appointed as God's servant to proclaim it. (Colossians 1:23 NLT)

Following Jesus and serving him as a slave are inseparable concepts. "Whoever serves me must follow me, and where I am, there will my servant be also," Jesus said (John 12:26). We cannot claim to be followers of Jesus while indulging our money-hungry, status-building, selfishly ambitious desires. "You are slaves of the one whom you obey," Paul told the Romans (Romans 6:16), and Paul advised those enslaved by the law (Galatians 3:23) or by their own desires (Romans 7:14) to allow Christ to purchase them (1 Corinthians 6:20), thus coming under a new and more excellent Master (1 Corinthians 7:22).

Some argue that by claiming to be a slave of Christ, Paul is actually esteeming and validating his ministry, since certain slaves of the Roman emperor were among the most powerful officials in the Empire.[4] And indeed if Christ is the Emperor of all emperors, being a servant in his household would mean a great deal. But I don't think that Paul's slavery language conjured up respect and nobility in the ears of his hearers. If slaves were so esteemed, then what was Spartacus's slave revolt all about? Moreover, for Jews, the two most defining moments were their liberation from slavery in Egypt in the exodus and their subjugation into slavery by the Assyrians and Babylonians in the exile. Jewish law made provision for Jews sold into slavery to fellow Israelites in order to insure their release with seven years (Deuteronomy 15:12-18). Slavery was not an esteemed metaphor among the Jews.

But don't think Paul, with his frequent use of *doulos* and *diakonos,* was referring to the oppressive nature of slavery as we've come to understand it in the West. My guess is that he assumed his readers would imagine a bond slave, a person who had become so beholden to another that he or she was bound to serve their benefactor in whatever way that person deemed useful. This un-American idea of being under someone else's rule—of not being captain of your own destiny—is what Paul intends for us to appreciate in his slave language.[5] And he not only uses it to describe his relationship with Jesus, but this former elitist (and possibly even slave owner at one time himself) also uses the notion of slavery to describe his relationship to others.

> For though I am free with respect to all, I have made myself a slave to all, so that I might win more of them.
> (1 Corinthians 9:19)

> For we do not proclaim ourselves; we proclaim Jesus Christ as Lord and ourselves as your slaves for Jesus' sake.
> (2 Corinthians 4:5)

Paul was so overcome by this Lover who would pursue the "chief of sinners" into the depths of hell that he could do no less than follow his Servant-King into the depths of servitude— servitude to Jesus and to the people whom Jesus loved, even those well "beneath" him. And Paul called churches to follow Christ onto this descending path of voluntary slavery: "For you were called to freedom, brothers and sisters; only do not use your freedom as an opportunity for self-indulgence, but through love become slaves to one another" (Galatians 5:13).

The posture of a slave has been associated with followers of Jesus from earliest times. Not only were many slaves in the first century drawn into the faith, but also believers who were free sold themselves as slaves in order to spread the gospel. In the oldest authentic Christian document outside the New Testament, the epistle of 1 Clement written to the Corinthian church (c. A.D. 96), the author speaks of free Corinthian believers selling themselves into slavery and using the proceeds to ransom others (1 Clement 55:2). And although unsuccessful, Moravian missionaries of the eighteenth century were willing to sell themselves into slavery in the West Indies in order to draw near to black slaves on sugar plantations.[6]

Instead of climbing corporate, political or even religious ladders, Paul guided Jesus' followers toward meekness by urging them to "lead a quiet and peaceable life in all godliness and dignity" (1 Timothy 2:2). When he speaks of spiritual gifts in 1 Corinthians 12—14 Paul gives precious little attention to the gifts of governing. Instead, he elevates love above all else—even above faith and hope! He was clear that Christians are not to be marked by selfish ambition and ascendency quests but by peace, kindness, teachability and patience with jerks: "A *doulos* [again, the Greek here is 'slave' but is euphemized in many translations to read 'servant'] of the Lord must not quarrel but must be kind to everyone, be able to teach, and be patient with difficult people" (2 Timothy 2:24 NLT). Ambition as we see it exercised in the world (and sometimes in the church) is turned on its head. Followers of Jesus should be preoccupied by an ambition to outdo one another in sacrificial love, respect, obedience and submission.

CHRIST: OUR SLAVE MENTOR

The high point of Paul's teaching on this love-inspired slavery mindset comes in his letter to the Philippians, where he says:

> Do nothing from selfish ambition or conceit, but in humility
> regard others as better than yourselves. Let each of you
> look not to your own interests,[7] but to the interests of others.
> Let the same mind be in you that was in Christ Jesus,
>
> > who, though he was in the form of God,
> > > did not regard equality with God
> > > as something to be exploited,
> > but emptied himself,
> > > taking the form of a slave,
> > > being born in human likeness.
> > And being found in human form,
> > > he humbled himself
> > > and became obedient to the point of death—
> > > even death on a cross. (Philippians 2:3-8)

In order to inspire the Philippians to set aside their selfish
quests for status, money or power and to take on a slave attitude,
Paul points to Jesus, who is King of kings yet willingly embraced
the form of a slave of slaves. If the Creator of the universe didn't
consider slavery beneath him, then how could his followers? "You
call me Teacher and Lord—and you are right, for that is what I
am," Jesus had told his disciples after washing their feet. "So if I,
your Lord and Teacher, have washed your feet"—slave's work—
"you also ought to wash one another's feet. For I have set you an
example, that you also should do as I have done to you. Very truly,
I tell you, servants [doulos] are not greater than their master"
(John 13:13-16).

What Jesus and Paul do when they hold up slavery as a model
for us is destroy a spirit of entitlement. Jesus, and to a certain
degree Paul, would have been justified in expecting that those
whom they taught would serve them in a variety of ways. But

when Jesus adopts the mindset of a slave by washing his followers' feet, or when Paul picks up a side-job so as not to be a financial burden on the people hosting him, they are exercising a slave mindset. A slave mindset says, "I'm not bothered that you've forgotten to wash my feet; in fact, I'll willingly wash yours." People who have chosen slavery out of love are free to give themselves to others without it damaging their ego or destroying their identity. They can sit on the curb with a mentally ill homeless person to share a sandwich, or cut their hours in order to take care of an aging parent, or move into a slum community in the developing world just to become loving neighbors to people whom the rest of the world has discarded. They can do this without being concerned about how it looks and without the false pride of thinking how great they are to stoop to such things. The slave mindset has freed them from an entitlement-spirit.

Cleaning up someone else's mess doesn't trip up a person who has the same mind that was in Christ when he emptied himself and cleaned up our mess. People with this sort of slave mindset can even take on leadership and responsibility in areas where no one else is willing to lead. They see a need and they step into it with neither pride nor grumbling because they're too motivated by love to worry about such things. When Jesus cooked breakfast for the disciples on the beach in John 21—after he had ascended to the Father and been crowned with glory—he didn't do it because he wanted to boast about how humble he was. And he certainly didn't do it out of a groveling, I'm-not-worthy, doormat insecurity. He did it because his friends needed to eat and because he loved them. It neither damaged nor inflated his ego to perform a task normally done by the lowest ranking person.

What's interesting is that when Paul writes to people with slave names in his letters, he often talks to them about their freedom in

Christ or refers to them as "fellow workers" and not as slaves.[8] He realized that they knew from experience how to humbly serve, so he didn't need to use the slave metaphor. But when speaking to free persons, he called them to embrace their new identity as a slave: "For whoever was called in the Lord as a slave is a freed person belonging to the Lord, just as whoever was free when called is a slave of Christ" (1 Corinthians 7:22).

Freely embracing our identity as a slave is important, because it's possible for a slave mindset to grow out of an unhealthy attitude of self-hatred or resignation. Among the extremely poor, for instance, it's rather common to find that they embrace poverty and servitude as their deserved destiny. They ought to be a poor rickshaw-puller or dumpsite scavenger because they don't deserve any better—or so their thinking goes. This is not the sort of perspective that Paul and Jesus were trying to inculcate in their use of slave language. Paul tells those serving as slaves, "Render service with enthusiasm, as to the Lord and not to men and women, knowing that whatever good we do, we will receive the same again from the Lord, whether we are slaves or free" (Ephesians 6:7-8; see also Colossians 3:22-24). Slave or master—neither counts for much in God's kingdom. What counts are things like service, obedience and submission offered freely, not because you have to but because you choose to. The slave mindset that Jesus embodied was voluntary, not coerced. It was motivated by love, not by fear. Therefore we serve even in the most undesirable positions out of confidence in our worth.

Although Paul was more concerned with the exercise of excellent servanthood than he was with excellent leadership, this is not to suggest that Paul forbade those in the church from exercising authority over each other. Paul intended that the followers of Christ be well governed by overseers.

EVIL DICTATORS AND CULT LEADERS

Paul wrote not only about servanthood in relation to Jesus and to one another. It is clear that his mindset of coming under others included those in authority, whether Christian or pagan. Paul writes in Romans, for instance, that "everyone must submit to governing authorities. For all authority comes from God, and those in positions of authority have been placed there by God" (13:1 NLT). But does taking on a slave mindset really mean we have to submit to authority when that authority is a religious kook like Joseph Kony of the Lord's Resistance Army in northern Uganda or a political megalomaniac like Adolf Hitler?

First let me say that some of us questioning Paul's words here are just trying to get out of submitting to a decent person with whom we disagree or who we simply do not like. Your boss or spouse or elder is not a reincarnation of Stalin, and that ticket you got for going "only" five miles over the speed limit was not a travesty of justice. Following Jesus into these places of obedience, submission and service is more likely to cause harm to your ego than harm to your body. Still, the question is a fair one. When Jesus says, "Do not resist an evil person" (Matthew 5:39 NLT), and Paul says, "Everyone must submit to governing authorities," are they telling us that, as slaves, we should do anything that anyone with any kind of power asks of us, no matter what?

For someone who spoke quite a bit about kindness, gentleness and self-control, Paul did not mince words when it came to self-proclaimed church authorities who were leading people away from the faith. When some men claiming leadership authority among the Galatians said that Gentile believers needed to submit to circumcision, Paul suggested that these so-called church leaders go and castrate themselves (Galatians 5:12)! Maybe that was just the old, pre-struck-by-love Paul talking, but the fact is that Paul took a pretty hard line against false teachers in many of his letters. He did not intend for us to succumb to false doctrine, even if it were delivered by a heavenly angel (Galatians 1:8).

When Jesus talked about obeying teachers of the law, he instructed his followers to obey their right teaching without imitating their screwed-up lives: "So practice and obey whatever they tell you, but don't follow their example. For they don't practice what they teach" (Matthew 23:3 NLT). Discernment is expected as we submit and obey. If we are spiritually blind and need the help of someone with spiritual sight, it's foolish for us to hold on to the elbow of someone who is equally blind and expect them to lead us to safety (see Matthew 15:14). Jesus and Paul encouraged thoughtful discernment before coming under the authority of a spiritual leader.

As far as state rulers were concerned, both Jesus and Paul were enough of a threat to the "governing authorities" that they were tried and executed by them. They advocated paying taxes and respecting those employed by the state, but they also introduced a kingdom with such radically different operating principles that Christians throughout history have been accused of subverting state authority by acknowledging that there is a Ruler whose commands trump state rulers. In fact, Jesus fully expected that those who take followership seriously would get into trouble with people in power. "But beware!" he said. "For you will be handed over to the courts and will be flogged with whips in the synagogues. You will stand trial before governors and kings because you are my followers" (Matthew 10:17-18 NLT). Missionaries are denied visas and Christians are imprisoned or martyred because the kingdom of God is a competing threat to governments that demand absolute devotion. But even under those kinds of governments, we're called to be submissive in our resistance. When Jesus said, "Do not resist an evil person," he used a word for "resist" which implies returning violence with violence.[9] It was not an encouragement to turn a blind eye to the abuse of power. It was a call to place a check on the warped human tendency to "fight fire with fire."

Our respect for authority, even when that authority is held by the unrighteous (remember, "there is no one who is righteous," Romans 3:10), can in fact unmask evil leaders when submission is undertaken out of choice and not out of fear. Jesus said, "No one can take my life from me. I sacrifice it voluntarily" (John 10:18 NLT). It is with this posture of volitional and willing submission that real power is displayed. Or, as Walter Wink puts it,

> by submitting to the authority of the Powers, Jesus acknowledged their necessity but rejected the legitimacy of their pretentious claims. He submitted to their power to execute him, but in so doing relativized, de-absolutized, de-idolized them, showing them to be themselves subordinate to the one who subordinated himself to them.[10]

To be forced by a Roman soldier to carry military gear for a mile, only to voluntarily offer to carry it for a second mile, places the meek in control. It says, "I don't serve you because I fear your authority or even your ability to kill me; I do it freely because I choose to. I take on this slave-nature of my own accord. I do it in imitation of a Master whose rule of 'two miles' overrides your rule of 'one mile.'"[11] And when one is slapped in the face, he or she places themselves in the driver's seat by offering the perpetrator the other cheek. Wink suggests that this is not only a counterintuitive, nonviolent way to oppose the abuse of power but is also actually effective in shaming the powerful by taking oppression a step further and exposing injustice for what it is. While I don't think that shaming those in power was the central point of Jesus' teaching to "turn the other cheek" (Matthew 5:39), I have seen for myself how the power of this meek approach can disarm a bully.

I was a bit of an outcast as a kid. Jimmy, who took the bus to and from school with me, was only slightly higher in his status as a middle-schooler than I was (though he was significantly taller). Probably because I was the only person he wasn't afraid of, he decided he was going to fight me at the bus stop in order to prove he could at least physically overpower one person. Twenty kids gathered in a circle as Jimmy began pushing and hitting. I kept telling him that I wasn't going to fight him, so I let him push me around and didn't hit back. With every push or punch that I didn't return he became more and more embarrassed. Finally he gave up and walked away in disgrace, having accomplished nothing more than lowering his status as someone who couldn't even beat a twerp under five feet tall. Please don't assign too much nobility to me; mostly I was just too scared to fight back! At the time it was incredibly humiliating, but looking back I see that Jimmy was the one who lost the most in the exchange. By voluntarily submitting to Jimmy's blows, he was utterly unable to prove his physical superiority over me. When the weak violently retaliate, they often simply cement the unjust use of authority by the strong.

Paul's message in Romans 13 to submit to governing authorities is not a call for blind submission to unjust rule. He is simply reminding the Roman believers that human authority exists on earth because God created it for our good. Or, as he tells the Colossians when he quotes an ancient Christian hymn, "whether thrones or dominions or rulers or powers—all things have been created through him and for him" (Colossians 1:16). Authority was created good, even though it can be misused. Again, Wink says it well:

> To say that the Powers are created in, through and for the cosmic Christ, then, does not imply endorsement of any particular economic or political system. What the hymn sings is recognition that it is God's plan for us to live in

interrelationship with each other, and to this end God has determined that there will be subsystems whose sole purpose is to serve the human needs of the One who exemplifies and encompasses humanity.[12]

Paul actually so revered governments that he preferred submitting to the harsh consequences of disobeying state powers than to attempting to overthrow them when they conflicted with God's authority. John Howard Yoder says, "The conscientious objector who refuses to do what his government asks him to do, but still remains under the sovereignty of that government and accepts the penalties which it imposes, . . . is being subordinate even though he is not obeying."[13]

Power was made by the triune God to be a guard for the weak, a check against the wicked, and to advance the welfare of all. To take on the mindset of a slave is to celebrate God's design that we are meant to place ourselves underneath others. The fact that it's possible for power to be abused must give us pause, but it doesn't mean we can disregard it whenever it's inconvenient to us or offends our personal preferences. Personal preference is secondary for a servant; obedience is primary. And when power is misused, Christ's servants willingly submit to a lashing for disobedience instead of to the desire to depose the powerful through violence. Oppression is an indication that power is broken and in need of healing, not useless and in need of elimination.

We have given ourselves too much license to reject authority we don't like under a moralizing guise. As slaves of Christ and as those who excel at following, we should submit to those in authority and to one another out of reverence for Christ—even when that authority is brandished by imperfect, fallible people with whom we do not agree. By the same token we must love authority enough to call it back to its holy purpose of guarding the weak and promoting the good of all when it has been co-opted as a tool for the powerful to accomplish their selfish designs. The easy path is to ignore authority when it's inconvenient to us, and to turn a blind eye to it when it's oppressive. A stance of humble submission and servanthood, where we esteem others above ourselves while still insisting on uncompromising justice, will surely become dangerous to the Christ-following servant—especially as we esteem those who are oppressed at the cost of our own comfort or well-being.

MY ORDINATION: A REMINDER OF MY BONDAGE

The line between a clear godly structure in a church and a dead institutional religiosity is a fine one. I am part of a congregation with no senior pastor. There are elders, housegroup leaders, teachers and worship leaders, and a few paid members who help administrate or devote their attention to our youth and children, but we have no "clergy" in the traditional sense. Still, I sensed that I had been called of God to fully give myself to an apostolic life on behalf of the global church. After puzzling over this with the elders, we decided to create an ordination process and a ceremony within our little, nondenominational church that might illustrate my call, something that acknowledged there was a spiritual covenant rather than a business contract in regard to my relationship to the broader church. The process of having my theology and character tested by people whom I respect, then pledging myself to Christ and his church, was sort of like getting hitched. It was the only vow I have ever made besides my marriage vow.

Parts of the ordination ceremony were . . . well . . . unconventional. Like the section of the service when the elders bound my hands and feet with rope and tied a blindfold that read "Holy to the Lord" over my eyes. Lest you think my ordination degenerated into some sort of fraternal hazing ritual, the elders associated this act of bondage in the physical realm with something that was happening spiritually through my ordination. "You are no longer your own," Paul Bell, one of the elders announced. "Your eyes are not your own, your hands and feet cannot act of their own accord, except under bondage to Christ and commitment to his church. In becoming ordained you give up your right to self-rule, out of love, and you pledge yourself to Christ and his church as a servant."

Slaves were often branded, so not long after getting ordained, I got a tattoo on the inside of my right wrist. It is a Coptic Christian cross, and I had it etched into me at a Coptic monastery in a poor community that collects and sorts through the refuse of Cairo, Egypt.[14] I had long marveled that Christ chose to retain the mutilation caused by his crucifixion when

Coptic Cross

he rose from the dead. It is a picture in his body of his submission to God and to the broken human authority that executed him— which he did for the sake of love. So I decided that if he could mark himself for me for all eternity, I could mark myself as a slave for him in this life (maybe I'll even get to keep the tattoo in the hereafter). What's more, I wanted somehow to express my covenant to the broader church and to the poor—things which are integral to my bond service. The Coptic garbage community in Cairo was one in which my family and I and a group of students lived in 2002. After returning several times, I felt a kindred spirit with the people there, and it seemed like the right place to express this covenant to Christ and to his global church. My tattoo and my ordination are marks in my body and my soul that I am a slave of Christ and of his church, and I was pleased to do both as an act of love.

PRACTICALLY A SLAVE

The physical obedience that comes with the attitude of a servant or a slave is the easy part. I usually don't have too much trouble doing what my elders or my boss tell me to do because of my compliant, middle-child nature. But to "regard others as better than yourselves," as Paul commands, is a serious challenge for me. Paul isn't necessarily talking about bosses, elders and emperors; he's talking about that attention-seeking, immature goof sitting on the bus (or in the pew) next to you. Without destroying our sense of self or ignoring the need for healthy boundaries, we must look at the unpleasant person next to us as many Asian cultures view their elders, or as the host in a home views the guest: with preferential esteem. We're to insist that they have the biggest piece of meat and sit in the nicest place. This is the slave mindset with which we need to approach others— especially those who treat us poorly if we take seriously Jesus' teaching about not just doing good to those who do good to you (Luke 6:33).

Education is the killer here for me. The "old self" doesn't seem to regard people without education as "better." It keeps telling me I'm better than them. This is one occupational hazard of working with the university world. I can be kind and attentive, hanging out with and listening to those with little education. I can wax eloquent about the difference between wisdom and education, calling others to value those who have no formal education but possess great life experience and real wisdom. But for me to take a developmentally disabled friend to the store with the attitude of a servant caring for a revered benefactor (especially if they are angry or hard to get along with) . . . that is something the old self just won't let me do. There is a lurking paternalism which prevents me from adopting the mind of Christ when I help people who (for instance) don't know where China is on a map.

When I talk with the mentally ill or the developmentally disabled, offering to pray with them, it is often with a subtle feeling that I am nobly helping a needier and less complete person. I have no problem looking up to the elders in my church, my boss at work or university students. But to take a homeless guy who can barely read to lunch without feeling like it's some humble act of condescension belies my blasted superiority complex and gets in the way of becoming like Christ the slave. I have been called to the carpet by mentally ill friends before. "Why is it that you offer to pray for me?" they've asked me. "Why don't you seek me out to pray for you? Is it because you believe you're better?" It's as if they can hear in my offer to pray a faint note of primacy.

I suppose there is a certain amount of servanthood involved in giving others my time, money, attention or physical strength. But if I'm honest, to really "regard others as better than yourself" in my heart, mind and soul—this is a place of deep struggle and profound failure. To learn the true spirit of a servant, I ought to look to the monastic communities who for centuries have slaved away for the least on earth, expecting no recognition or repayment. This amazing ability to serve those whom no one else cares about is due in part to their willingness to come under the strict authority of a fellow brother or sister.

SEVEN

OBEDIENCE AND THE
DEATH OF INDEPENDENCE

Would I rather be feared or loved?" asks Michael
Scott, regional manager of Dunder-Mifflin, a micro-cap paper
regional distributor featured in the TV comedy *The Office*. "Both," he
concludes. "I want people to be afraid of how much they love me."

The Office is a wildly successful rip-off TV series (copied from a
British show of the same name) that offers a humorous window on
corporate life through the eyes of employees who give documentary-like
commentary to the goings-on in their office. It is the manager, Michael's,
idiocy that makes the show so much fun to watch. It's funny to see
intelligent, capable workers being supervised by a buffoon who has no
business being in a position of authority over others. Maybe we enjoy
watching because of the feeling of vindication that wells up, since most
of us believe we could do a better job than the incompetent supervisor
over us. (Note to my supervisor: This isn't the case in our relationship. I
think you're a great boss . . . but then, I suppose I'm a bit like Dwight.)

I find this attitude especially rampant in those of us born and raised in the United States—this smug posture of superiority, playing the martyr underling who bears up under the unjust rule of someone who is half the person we are. And with each generation the feeling grows. More and more we seem to love stories that portray people in authority as cruel or insensitive or, as in the case of Michael Scott, as imbeciles. I cannot imagine a Japanese TV series, for instance, becoming popular because it purposely exaggerates the stupidity of a person in authority in order to lampoon supervisors.

The movie *The Madness of King George* (1994) is about the reign of British monarch King George III who ruled England from 1760 to 1801. In the movie, as in the real-life story of King George III, the king slips into periods of severe insanity, now believed to have been triggered by the blood disease porphyria. He becomes incapable of dispatching the duties of a king, yet because of his royal position, those around him kowtow to his demented behavior. This is the king whose tea tax inspired the Boston Tea Party and whose shackles were cast off by American colonists in the 1770s. Is it any wonder that Americans have such a disdain for those in authority? America's founders suffered under the reign of a madman, and the immigrants who followed them were motivated by a desire to break free of their own religious or political overlords. White American culture has inherited this anti-authoritarian DNA.

YOU'RE NOT THE BOSS OF ME

Even though eighteenth-century Americans were glad to jettison their monarch, they still had comparatively high regard for people with authority. In those days, you were employed as an apprentice, and you obeyed even the most menial commands of your master. A young man had to ask permission of a young woman's father before proposing marriage. A professor was addressed as a sort of lord. Priests and pastors held a level of power over a congregation that would probably be considered illegal today. Most Americans said "yes sir" and "yes ma'am" to people ascribed with authority (the terms *sir* and *ma'am* are still in use today, but only in a very limited geographical band approximately fifty miles wide running between Johnson City, Tennessee, and Yulee, Georgia).

But the authority-resistant gene was in the pool, and each generation has amplified it. The respectful attitude toward some forms of power which existed two hundred years ago has all but disappeared today. "You're not the boss of me!" is one of the first phrases I learned as a kid playing with others. If we don't like a rule or the person laying down the rule, then we take our ball and go elsewhere. Americans have been some of the best at splitting off into new denominations, though this has changed in recent years. Now we're so tired of creating new religious leadership structures every time we run into Michael Scott types that we've pretty much done away with inventing new denominations. When evangelicals begin churches nowadays, they tend to be like my church: little, independent congregations that are more or less answerable to no one. Part of what attracted Janine and me to our little fellowship was our desire to come out from under an institutional church structure which did not permit us the freedom we desired. Numerous churches use the word *free* or *independent* in their titles as a badge to indicate they have no institutional oversight.

Those of us who consider ourselves part of avant-garde emerging church communities that have been born out of the budding twenty-first-century reformation revel in the biblical examples of confrontations with authority, such as Jesus turning the tables in the temple and John the Baptist preaching against King Herod. And to be sure, there is something subversive about this kingdom destined to be inherited by the meek in a world that tends to reward the rich and powerful. But the truth is that we were designed by God to obey others.

When God told the first humans to have dominion over every living thing that moves on the earth (Genesis 1:28), I think he probably had communities of people in mind as well as other creatures. This was not a call for exploitation and domination; it was a mantle of governance and stewardship—a call to exercise the creativity and authority of God over one another and the earth in a way that would promote the flourishing of creation and the welfare of the weak. We were regents of the Creator, commissioned to benevolent rule and, by extension, commissioned to be ruled by one another. Obedience was expected to be a normal part of life on earth.

One of the first images of leadership and governance in the Bible is that of shepherd; it's how Moses refers to his successor, Joshua (Numbers 27:17), and how God refers to the leaders of Israel (2 Samuel 7:7; Jeremiah 23:1-4). The same metaphor is used to describe the authority and care of God himself (Psalm 23), and Christ uses it to describe his relationship to his followers (John 10). It is telling that God would use the same picture of a humble animal caretaker (shepherds, by the way, did not have high status; see Genesis 46:34) to illustrate both his authority over humans and human authority over one another. It's another indication that our rulership over one another is meant to resemble God's rulership over us, a rulership which cares for the lost, the strays, the injured and the weak and which brings the staff of judgment to bear upon the wolves of oppression. In fact, when Jesus referred to himself as the good shepherd in John 10 he was borrowing from the Old Testament passage in Ezekiel where God chides the shepherds of Israel for their abuse of the sheep and promises a righteous shepherd who will guard against exploitation.

I myself will be the shepherd of my sheep, and I will make them lie down, says the Lord GOD. I will seek the lost, and I will bring back the strayed, and I will bind up the injured, and I will strengthen the weak, but the fat and the strong I will destroy. I will feed them with justice. (Ezekiel 34:15-16)

In Christian circles I sometimes hear the metaphor of shepherds touted as an illustration of leadership and spoken of in reference to growing our ability to exercise authority over others. While this is a useful image for leaders, I've noticed that almost nobody uses this agrarian illustration to speak about the need for all of us to become good sheep, because that would require talking about the value of obedience. Obedience is only for well-behaved men and women, and we all know that "well-behaved women never make history." It's a bumper sticker so it must be true.

Well-behaved, obedient and *submissive* are all insulting adjectives in America, unless speaking about a child or a dog. The popular kids cartoon *SpongeBob SquarePants* depicts SpongeBob as excessively compliant and all-too-eager to obey his employer, Mr. Crab. But it is his obedient nature which is buffoonized in the series. His hapless obedience makes him such a lovable, innocent idiot, and while we'd all like SpongeBob as a friend, none of us wants to be like him. But obedience is a prerequisite to good following—something that is profoundly critical to good shepherding. Even the great king David put himself in the place of the sheep when he wrote his famed Psalm 23.

Isaiah 53:6 states that we all like sheep have gone astray; everyone has turned to self-leadership. This is the ultimate prophetic accusation of human depravity and sin. Our anti-authoritarian arrogance insists we are most free to be ourselves when we answer to nobody and shows up in our tendency to shun obedience to someone with whom we disagree. When we're asked to do something we don't want to at work, we leave our jobs. When we don't like our pastors or elders or worship leaders, we leave our churches. When we don't like our teachers, we drop our classes. When we don't like something a friend tells us, we stop listening to them. And when we don't find sex enjoyable or when we tire of squeezing toothpaste from the bottom up, we leave our spouses. Freeing ourselves from authority is extolled because we worship freedom and individualism. After all, who would want to commit themselves to a relationship where you must regularly die to personal freedom and independence in favor of someone else's idea of life and work?

It turns out that the monastic community would. Their existence celebrates sheep-likeness and submission.

WED TO POVERTY, CHASTITY AND OBEDIENCE

In September 1946, the voice of Jesus pleaded with thirty-six-year-old Sister Mary Teresa on a Darjeeling retreat, "Come, come, carry me into the holes of the poor. Come be My Light."[1] Mother Teresa understood this appeal to be a change in her present missionary career educating young girls on the pristine grounds of St. Mary's School for Girls; she knew she was to go into the desperate slums of Calcutta. It was a call to satiate the thirst of Jesus for the poor. "There are convents with numbers of nuns caring for the rich and able to do people," the voice urged, "but for my very poor there is absolutely none. For them I long—them I love—Wilt thou refuse?"[2]

What made this invitation particularly weighty was a vow Mother Teresa had taken just a few years prior. "With permission of my confessor, I made a vow to God—binding under mortal sin—to give God anything that He may ask—'Not to refuse Him anything.'"[3] In a sense, Mother Teresa told God, "If I ever refuse you anything, then damn me to hell." She had wanted to give him something beautiful, and after considering this seriously and discussing it with her confessor, she had concluded that this vow, this permanent "yes" to God, was the most beautiful thing she had to give.

But Mother Teresa was bound by oath to obey her human superiors, and they needed time to test this call. The seeming conflict between her oath to obey Jesus in all things and her covenant commitment to her order created excruciating anguish as this call of Christ to the poor was pondered and questioned, first by her spiritual director and then by the archbishop of Calcutta. "I beg of you your Grace, in the Name of Jesus and for the love of Jesus to let me go. Delay no longer. Keep me not back," she pleaded to the archbishop, nearly a year after Jesus had beckoned her into the slums.

Mother Teresa,
photo by Evert Odekerken

But Mother Teresa was committed to strict obedience to her superiors. She was not free to act as a "Rambo" nun, bucking authority, gathering other spiritual vigilantes and rushing into the slums with her holy bazooka. Even with the voice of Jesus himself calling her, she was bound to honor what was deemed appropriate by those above her. Such is the life she had abandoned herself to, a life of complete obedience to the will of her overseers, despite any personal preference or internal suffering that submission to their orders might bring. The human voice would be the final authority in testing the divine voice. Mother Teresa was convinced that by giving herself over to the authority of the church, God's true desires would be borne out through the decision of her superiors. Of course, if they were wrong, they would bear before God the responsibility and judgment of their decision—a fact that she reminded the archbishop of when she submitted this call to him.

At one point in this trial of submission, the voice of Jesus addressed the issue of monastic obedience. Of the archbishop, Jesus said to his "little one" (as he sometimes referred to Mother Teresa in his divine exchanges), "Trust him completely and without any fear. Obey him in every detail, you shall not be deceived if you obey for he belongs to me completely.—I shall let you know my will through him."[4]

Protestants for the most part take or leave the advice of their spiritual overseers; fidelity to Scriptures and our own interpretation of them trumps all else. The potentially conflicting position that Mother Teresa (or any who take vows within a Roman Catholic order) faced was a pledge of fidelity to God and to Scripture and yet resignation to obey very human and fallen spiritual supervisors. Obedience to human authority is woven into the fabric of monastic devotion to God. It is in the crucible of such submission that monks and nuns believe the will of God is revealed.

From the earliest days of monastic communities, obedience has been an unavoidable part of the package. St. Benedict is credited with bringing order to the medieval frenzy of creating religious communities, and obedience was one of the foundational commitments to which those who aspired to live a set-apart religious life had to adhere. In essence, if you're looking for leadership models that espouse democratic values, encourage independence or model decision-making by consensus, then don't look to monasteries or convents. To join such a community was to denounce your own will and become dead to any possibility for self-governance. According to Benedict, once an order was issued by the abbot, the monk was to attend to it without delay, "as if the matter had been commanded by God himself."[5] And Francis claimed that a corpse was the best picture of obedience, for "[a corpse] does not resent being moved, nor grumble at the place it is put, nor want back the place it left. . . . That is your true obedient person."[6]

Isn't this level of obedience destined to give rise to destructive abuses of power, with domineering superiors like Donald Trump or idiots like Michael Scott? And wouldn't the people drawn to them be sniveling insecure individuals or unthinking worshipers of anyone with a title? Sometimes, I suppose. And there certainly have been ecclesiastical abuses of power (not limited to Catholic orders, however). But for the most part monastic obedience has produced amazing fruit. The monastic orders of Europe are credited with saving civilization and ushering in (or at least keeping alive) the most accomplished art, the most prolific literature and the most rigorous schools on earth. Under the tutelage of monks and nuns have come some of the world's most productive scientists, writers, thinkers, artists and leaders. In fact, most of today's institutions of higher learning can directly or indirectly trace their genesis to a religious community which had obedience as a central tenet of its existence.

Imbedded in a religious order's call to obedience is the conviction that humans have an uncanny ability to deceive themselves. We can no more achieve real discipline, virtue and spiritual growth on our own than a person can rappel down the side of a cliff with both ends of the rope tied around their waist (technically, I suppose you could rappel like this, but only once, and very, very quickly). Women and men need to be anchored to someone outside themselves, someone who is committed to truth and who feels the moral weight of their office.

Benedict not only warned rebellious monks of the "crushing doom" of eternal death, but he also spoke of the "dread judgment of God" for an abbot who gave false teaching or made ungodly demands of those under him. The blame for the spiritual flabbiness of the flock or stray sheep would lie squarely with the shepherd. One of the reasons cult leaders are so dangerous is that they typically have no accountability. Benedict expected superiors to seek the counsel of the community, even the counsel of young monks, since "the Lord often reveals what is better to the younger."[7] And abbots were encouraged to offer hospitality to visiting monks and open themselves to "reasonable criticisms and observations," since Benedict believed God may have guided the visitor to the monastery for the purpose of offering a corrective word.

In monastic orders, those under authority could not, even at the insistence of a superior, do something contrary to a clear command of Scripture. Dominican monk and theologian St. Thomas Aquinas says in his *Summa Theologica,* "Sometimes the things commanded by a superior are against God. Therefore superiors are not to be obeyed in all things."[8] Basic discernment and devotion to the Word of God was expected of monks and nuns. Superiors were not charged with inventing new editions to God's revelation, but were expected to admonish their community to live out the existing revelations faithfully, not only in word, but also by the example of their deeds.

Monastic celebration of submission and sheep-likeness, then, was not an invitation to unthinking obedience, but obedience tempered by prayer, Scripture and discernment. Obedience was made more secure by the seriousness with which superiors exercised their leadership, gravely understanding the judgment that befalls those in authority. And they were pledged to submission as well, submission to the authority of the wider community and to the rule of their order.

OBEDIENCE WITHOUT AN ATTITUDE

Cults are for automatons unwilling to think for themselves, and the destiny of the "free spirit" is spiritual stagnation since they refuse to come under any master. It takes a person of real self-confidence to follow unwaveringly an imperfect, broken leader without grumbling.

Benedict demanded not only the external obedience of submitting to an abbot's orders but also the internal obedience of doing so without complaining, something Thomas Merton struggled with throughout his life as a Trappist monk. Like Augustine, Merton lived a wild life before committing himself to a monastic existence. But as a monk Merton became one of the most fertile Catholic writers and thinkers of his day. One of the curses of being so intelligent and deeply spiritual was how hard it made it to follow the requirement of submitting to people who were sometimes less intelligent or spiritually inept. Of his Father Abbot in 1959 Merton journaled, "He is certainly as unscrupulous as any politician can be, and will not stop at anything—as long as it can be made to *appear* fair."[9] He refers to one of his Reverend Fathers as a "sentimental prima donna," journaling on and on with exasperation at being placed under his unspiritual, bureaucratic tendencies: "He is one of the most neatly compartmentalized minds I know of. To your face, gushing with affection. In another context, behind your back, laughing at your idiosyncrasies with some other officer. In public, demonstrating a great interest in your work. In private, despising it completely."[10] But Merton obeyed. He had to; he was a monk. To him, obedient submission under someone like Michael Scott was of greater value than leaving the order in a self-righteous tizzy simply because he was right.

Merton's greatest test of obedience was the silencing demanded by his superiors when he began to write against nuclear war in the 1960s. He wrote an entire book, *Peace in the Post-Christian Era,* just before the gag order and offered to submit the work to the Trappist censors in order to make it acceptable. The French Abbot General in Rome, Dom Gabriel Sortais, wrote back, unmoved: "Abstain from writing in any way whatsoever about the subject of nuclear war." Merton dutifully obeyed but inwardly bristled at the notion that his superiors believed speaking for peace somehow gave monasticism a bad name.

During this trying period Merton wrote, "A spirit that is drawn to God in contemplation will soon learn the value of obedience. . . . The most dangerous man in the world is the contemplative guided by nobody."[11] In time, many of his writings promoting peace were released by the church, but not before testing the quality of Merton's vow of obedience.

DEATH OF INDEPENDENCE

I mentioned John David and Heidi earlier. They are committed to living in a Middle Eastern slum because they believe Jesus has called them there to bring spiritual life and material transformation to the Muslim poor. Because of the complications, suspicions and challenges of a young American couple moving into a Muslim slum, it took nearly two years and several false starts to secure their slum apartment. Only weeks after they had finally moved in and begun developing relationships, they were scheduled by their mission organization, Servant Partners, to come back to the U.S.

for a team leaders' conference. "Coming to the U.S. at this stage would set us back months, once you take into account the disengagement that comes in the preparation process, the actual weeks in the U.S. and the time it takes to adjust after we return," John David confided. So they appealed to their supervisor, asking permission to skip the conference. Their supervisor asked a few questions, prayed and consulted others. In time, he came to the conclusion that they should return to the U.S. for this leaders' event. John David and Heidi disagreed with the decision, but they came anyway. It was costly. Not only did they pay the price of losing irreplaceable weeks of integration into their new neighborhood, but they also paid the emotional price of moving back and forth between privilege and deprivation. John David writes,

> We walked towards the bridge that spans the sewage canal and railroad tracks that separate the lives and homes of the very poor from the very rich. We walked across this bridge and got into a taxi we had waiting on us to drive us to the airport to board our flights. . . . The tickets for these flights cost the equivalent of our slum apartment's rent, and our neighbor's rent, for *six full years.*
>
> Within an hour we went from our slum apartment and our neighbors who have no concept whatsoever of what it would be like to even dream of boarding a plane to fly to a foreign land, to the country's international airport where a can of Coca-Cola costs more than what Heidi and I and our neighbors, spend on food for *three entire days!*
>
> We boarded our flight and journeyed, from one extreme to another, from one world to another. Our lives are lived in extremes, and we find ourselves having to move between two very different worlds as we, privileged, wealthy,

educated Americans, attempt to incarnate ourselves amongst the very poor, identifying with them in their sufferings, and freely choosing poverty in order to live alongside of them. We move from wealth to voluntary poverty, from seasons of being surrounded by other believers and followers of Christ, to seasons of nearly total isolation; from lifestyles of ease and plenty, to the regular daily discomforts and deprivations of the world's poor. And yet in comparison to the incredible act of God's incarnation, this is nothing.[12]

John David and Heidi came back to the States at the request of their supervisor with an eagerness to contribute to and learn from others at the conference. They respected their supervisor with whom they disagreed. They had voluntarily tethered themselves to a mission with a structure, and they undertook submission as an act of worship.

Weeks later, when they returned to their slum, it was apparent that the secret police had come into the apartment and rifled through all their possessions, searching for incriminating information to use in order to deport them. Within six months they had been kicked out of the country. Whether it would have been positive or negative in the long run for them to have remained in the Middle East during the conference is not clear. What is clear to me is that they will benefit from the trust that was built and the selfishness that was destroyed in their act of obedience. They are learning to tame the independent, maverick American spirit and become true servants, willingly placing themselves under the direction of men and women whom they respect, but who they sometimes disagree with.

One of the stated values of Servant Partners reads a bit like a monastic rule: "We will seek to die to ourselves in all areas of life: finances, possessions, housing, decision-making, and ministry opportunities. We will live sacrificially for one another in our relationships and in our marriages. We will seek to submit to one another in love. We will seek wisdom from God and from one another in exercising this principle."[12] It is this communal dependence, this wrestling self-will to the ground to undertake sheep-like obedience, that gives true freedom for growth.

PRACTICALLY OBEDIENT

On a mission trip to Mexico City, my daughter Hannah was attempting to mediate the messiness of relationships in crisis back home via email and Facebook. There is something draining and unsatisfying about working out problems over cyberspace, and she soon realized that she was powerless to do much from where she sat in Mexico City.

"God," she prayed, "help me to know what to do."

"Will you do what I tell you?" came his reply.

"What do you want me to do?" Hannah needed a bit more detail before saying yes.

"Will you do what I ask?" God replied again.

"How can I know unless you tell me what it is?" Hannah wondered.

"I want your 'yes,' " God said, "before you know what I will ask of you."

Hannah later said that she didn't believe God had a specific command in mind with regard to her friends. It was simply his response to her prayer, as if he were saying, "Why ask me what to do if you do not intend to do it?"

Now, I should tell you that Hannah is easily one of the most independent people I know. She was ready to move out and live on her own at age eleven. An unconditional "yes" to God was a profound challenge for this highly autonomous eighteen-year-old. Could she trust him enough to give him a "yes" before knowing what he would ask?

A week later, Hannah and the rest of us were spending time in an impoverished community, building relationships and hanging out with mostly single moms who were on a journey from desperation to stability. They were on this road thanks to a transformational Christian ministry known as Armonia (which means "harmony," or "shalom" in Spanish). We listened to the founder, Saul Cruz, tell the story of how he and his wife, Pilar, began this work among the poorest of Mexico City's urban poor thirty years prior.

Shortly after graduating from seminary, Saul delivered a stinging sermon at a friend's church on the call of Christ to serve the poor. Afterward, a rich lawyer in the congregation grabbed Saul and cryptically said, "Come with me." At first Saul wondered if he was going to be verbally assaulted by this wealthy man. When the lawyer shoved Saul into his Cadillac and brought him to an area of the city that Saul never knew existed, he wondered if there might even be a physical assault in store for him.

The area was home to an impoverished community living off of refuse, like too many similar communities in the cities of the developing world. Saul was deeply disturbed to see the plight of these desperately poor people. He ordered the lawyer to stop the car when he noticed a naked child the age of his toddler son eating from a mound of rotting trash. It undid him.

It turns out that the lawyer hadn't brought Saul there to unload on him verbally or physically; he had brought him there to unload a piece of property on him. The lawyer confided that God had led him to this garbage community and, like with Mother Teresa, had urged him to personally care for the people there. "It is too hard for me to obey. I cannot do it," he told Saul, "so I have brought you here to do the thing that I cannot bring myself to do." He deeded over to Saul a plot of ground he had purchased in this garbage community and walked away from sheep-like submission and obedience.

Saul and Pilar decided they could not live the sanitized life of middle-class church leaders after seeing such squalor; they couldn't walk away from this plot of rubbish. Now, through their character and their thirty years of ministry to the poor, Hannah and the rest of us on the team got to see both the price and the reward of saying yes to God. As Hannah considered their obedience, God's call to give him a standing "yes" a week earlier imbedded itself in her soul. A blank check of obedience is something she is now attempting to live out in spite of her defiant, independent personality.

This kind of absolute trust is hard to give to God, let alone humans. Our desire to be in control is overpowering at times. We will sometimes submit to God because we know it's the right thing to do and because he is God, after all. Submitting to another person can be significantly more challenging. It involves obeying someone—likely someone who isn't like you, maybe even someone with "issues"—and that implies dependence. Submission through obedience to a person is a resignation of self-control and an admission that we need others. And submission to someone we perceive as inferior to us feels just plain wrong. But the fact that most of us struggle with pride means there will almost always be people we consider inferior in authority over us.

Paul urges us in Ephesians 5:21 to "submit to one another out of reverence for Christ" (NIV). Another way to put it might be, "Since you respect and trust Jesus, set down your independence and obey people in your community. This will really please him."

It is very challenging to put independence to death and embrace healthy submission and obedience if you don't live in some sort of community, whether community formed by marriage or birth or simply by common vision and purpose. The only thing God declared "not good" in all of the beauty of his creation was the aloneness of Adam before Eve. We are designed to be in a state of dependence, not independence. Whether in our living situation, our working situation or in our pursuit of education, we cannot grow or be complete if we don't submit to, depend on and obey others. We were never meant to rule ourselves.

What would it look like if we really undertook submission and obedience to others as an act of worship and a path to spiritual growth, even if it were submission and obedience to people who were broken and weak like Michael Scott? What if we obeyed our teachers and bosses so long as they were not asking us to murder or deny Christ? What if we submitted to our worship leaders even when we didn't feel like worshiping? What if we submitted to those who have spiritual authority because they are our spiritual directors, our pastors or our elders? What if we submitted to those who have civic authority because they are in office (even if I didn't vote for them)? And what if we gave these people real obedience? Not pick-only-the-decisions-I-like obedience, or I'm-just-going-to-make-it-look-like-I'm-obeying obedience, or even I'll-do-it-but-with-a-bad-attitude obedience. What if we gave those around us the kind of obedience that believes there is virtue in dying to self and to our preferences, and that there is beauty in preferring and esteeming others?

To take submission and obedience deeper, what if our submission and obedience were done in a spirit of repentance that worked its way through our bank accounts and made its way to the margins of society? What if we sought downward mobility through this submission and obedience, not troubling ourselves about the potential loss of status? Submission like that would not require comparison to others. We'd be free to listen to God and devote ourselves to whatever path he set us on. It would allow us the freedom to offer ourselves as slaves to others voluntarily, without destroying our sense of worth or becoming a doormat. Submission and obedience like that might kill the old self and grow meekness. It might even make the Michael Scott types in authority over us better leaders. Even if it doesn't, I believe it will make you and me more like the One who submitted to us, even to the point of death, in order that we might have real life. And becoming more like him might just be worth the risk of giving our respectful obedience to the Michael Scotts of our lives.

EIGHT

MEEKNESS AND THE NEED FOR TRUE LEADERSHIP

Janine and I were housegroup leaders at church during a very turbulent time in the life of our body. We were charged with caring for a small band of people who met every Sunday night, but a series of changes in our fellowship led to widespread discontent. When people shared their heartaches and troubles, most concerns centered on our church and how poorly it was being led. Sunday nights became an opportunity to complain about the shifting values of our church.

In time, some from our small group got so upset that they stopped attending the worship service on Sunday morning but continued coming on Sunday nights for housegroup. They had lost faith in the elders yet wanted to remain connected to the church small group with whom they had built deep relationships. It was agonizing for Janine and me to lead a group which was supposed to be an extension of our fellowship but which had instead become a gathering of individuals angry with the church. Some began regularly attending other congregations. Janine and I weren't always sure ourselves about some of the decisions our church leaders were making, and even when we did feel good about a particular change of direction, change is such a messy affair that it rarely rolls out well. There is no clean and agreeable way to effect change.

The most painful thing Janine and I have done as church leaders was to call those in our housegroup either to be fully on board with our fallible church made up of fallible leaders who make fallible decisions, or to fully join the other churches they were attending and become part of small groups there. Over the course of about six months to a year, ten people left our small group. Janine and I chose to stay, and sticking with and submitting to this sometimes bungling body of believers has been both the most difficult and most rewarding voluntary interdependence we have developed. It's been an exercise of humility and meekness for us to engage the process of discussion and debate without pressing the fact that we believe we're right to the point of division, separation or abandoning ship.

CARVING UP JESUS' BODY

Too often with schisms in the church, a theological guise is used to hide what essentially is a power or personality struggle. Paul urged the bickering Corinthian church to "live in harmony with each other. Let there be no divisions in the church. Rather, be of one mind, united in thought and purpose" (1 Corinthians 1:10 NLT). The Corinthians were lining up, some behind Paul, some behind Peter, some siding with Apollos and some (a few purists) saying they didn't follow mere human leaders but only Christ. "Has Christ been divided into factions?" Paul asks (1 Corinthians 1:13 NLT).

Factions have plagued the followers of Jesus from the very beginning, carving up the body of Christ as if it were a piece of property instead of a living thing. Among the Corinthians, prestige was assigned to various believers based on which Christian celebrity they followed, or better yet, who baptized them. If you were brought to faith by the testimony of Apollos then baptized and discipled by him, the fans of Paul or Peter might seem foolish to you. We're not so different today. "Evangelicals bug me." "Catholics are idiots." "Pentecostals are weird." Of course most of the time we're more sophisticated in our denunciations of other believers. But these statements are windows to the arrogance in our souls. Jesus said, "It is out of the abundance of the heart that the mouth speaks" (Luke 6:45). When we slam others we're indicating our preference for pride over meekness, our penchant for comparison over following, and our mindset of spiritual entitlement over servanthood. For those who claim to follow Jesus, these statements are evidence of our choice not to love—and therefore, a show of blatant disobedience.

One of the differences between demons and disciples in the Gospels was that demons actually obeyed Jesus! Jesus commanded demons to leave and they did. But in regard to the two places where Jesus used the word *commandment* with the same sort of authority used in referring to the Old Testament commandments, the church has clearly been insubordinate. John 13:34 says, "So now I am giving you a new commandment: Love each other. Just as I have loved you, you should love each other" (NLT), and John 15:12 says, "This is my commandment, that you love one another as I have loved you."

Love. It is the thing that holds meekness, submission and repentance together. Love permeates the slave mindset and grants power for the follower and strength for the obedient. Love is both the first and second greatest commandment (Mark 12:28-31). That is why hate-laced divisions that carve up Jesus' body have always been and will ever be the greatest tragedy of Christ-followers.

One of the earliest and most vicious church divisions was the split that occurred between East and West, spawned by the forceful personalities of Cyril of Alexandria and Nestorius of Constantinople. Nestorius was a relatively obscure priest who was probably promoted too quickly to the office of Patriarch of Constantinople because of his great preaching abilities. This was a thorn in the craw of ambitious Cyril, who had been stewing ever since Constantinople bumped Alexandria out of the spot for most important patriarchate after Rome. Their struggle was essentially the same as the age-old power quest of James and John attempting to nuzzle Peter out and get the prime spots at Jesus' left and right hand. This ascendancy pursuit suppresses the call of Jesus to love one another, and the church suffers the consequences. Although both Cyril and Nestorius believed that Christ was fully divine and fully human, the theological rhetoric behind their warring vitriol was more about how one spoke about or emphasized Christ's humanity or his deity. Each side maligned and exaggerated what the other was saying in order to garner support.

St. Cyril of Alexandria. **Icon from the Convent of Saint Elizabeth**

The controversy blew up in one of the most embarrassing church councils in history, the Council of Ephesus in A.D. 431. Cyril demanded a council be convened to settle the debate. Then, when the bishops supporting Nestorius were delayed in arriving, Cyril took advantage of the favorable odds and called for a vote, promptly excommunicating Nestorius and settling the matter. However, Nestorius, knowing he would not get a fair hearing without his bishops, refused to attend or recognize the council until his delegation arrived. Tensions boiled over and those who supported Cyril "went about the city girt and armed with clubs . . . with the yells of barbarians, snorting fiercely. . . . They blocked up the streets so that everyone was obliged to flee and hide, while they acted as masters of the situation, lying about, drunk and besotted and shouting obscenities."[1]

Unfortunately, some of our church meetings today have just as much zest as the Council of Ephesus did. In fact, on November 9, 2008, a fistfight broke out at the Church of the Holy Sepulchre in Jerusalem between Greek Orthodox and Armenian monks. The embarrassing brawl was even caught on film.[2] (So much for monks being a perfect example of how to live the life of meekness and obedience.)

All too often church leaders and followers have positioned themselves like competing political parties, utterly convinced of the rightness of their position and ready to pounce upon anyone who thinks otherwise. Except for the occasional incident like the one that occurred at the Church of the Holy Sepulchre, most church fights today are accomplished simply by discrediting and ridiculing rival brothers and sisters rather than physically pummeling them. But either way, the power dynamics which operate in the MONOPOLY™ kingdoms of this world continue to plague the followers of Jesus with disastrous results. Taking up sides behind Paul or Peter, Cyril or Nestorius, evangelical or mainline, Democrat or Republican is pretty much the same in nature. Love is subordinated to arrogance rather than the other way around.

We are passionate people who like to make big deals over small differences, and it feels to us like resignation when we put these differences aside in honor of Christ's call for meekness, love and unity. Most disputes seem to us to be a matter of truth and justice while we're embroiled in them. What makes it all even more tragic, however, is the way we whitewash our hatred of one another in high-minded doctrinal language.

The sad truth is that much of our divisiveness and hatred is drummed up by those who have leadership gifts and a shepherd's calling. They are men and women who love authority more than they fear it.

AMONG YOU IT WILL BE DIFFERENT

When God set up the governing structure of Old Testament Israel he called for a plurality of leaders without a prime minister, president or king. He didn't install a senate as the core body of national decision makers but expected Israel to be led by judges (both men and women) who were appointed to guard against oppression and injustice.

> You shall appoint judges and officials throughout your tribes, in all your towns that the LORD your God is giving you, and they shall render just decisions for the people. You must not distort justice; you must not show partiality; and you must not accept bribes, for a bribe blinds the eyes of the wise and subverts the cause of those who are in the right. Justice, and only justice, you shall pursue, so that you may live and occupy the land that the LORD your God is giving you. (Deuteronomy 16:18-20)

In God's politics, multiple judges were to rule a nation rather than a single head of state. This was a statement about the central role he felt justice should occupy in society. He knew that justice was much more likely to be carried out in a nation run by a plurality of judges whose primary task was simply to insure that the law—a law which had a lot to do with protecting the poor, the alien, the fatherless and the widow—was followed. By contrast, a singular king would consolidate power, wealth and status into the hands of a specific person, placing the ego in jeopardy. This is why the meek will inherit the earth; they're more concerned with justice, particularly justice for the powerless, than they are with their own status.

When the Israelites eventually insisted on a king, the judge, Samuel, took it personally. But God told him, "Listen to the voice of the people in all that they say to you; for they have not rejected you, but they have rejected me from being king over them" (1 Samuel 8:7). God knew that his people would succumb to comparison when they entered the land and that they'd want to choose a king like everyone else. God's law permitted them to anoint a king, but Deuteronomy describes kingship in a radically different form than any monarchy I've heard about, and so far as I know, Israel never attained the relatively egalitarian vision of a king laid out for them in the law. For example, the king was forbidden to accumulate horses, wives or wealth. He was to read the law on a daily basis so that he would fear God and obey his commands. What's more, the king was warned against "exalting himself above other members of the community" (Deuteronomy 17:14-20).

God did not want political celebrities to govern his people. If the people wouldn't accept being ruled by the judicial branch of government without a single supreme ruler, if they insisted on an executive branch with a chief executive, then that person was not to have an exalted status. The king was to be like common folk. It would be an exercise of leadership through meekness, insuring the death of pride. God insisted that the nation's leader not succumb to the accumulation of money and the inflation of status. The same was to be true of leaders in the church. The New Testament uses different words for leaders to depict different types of leadership. The word *archōn,* for example, is used to describe a ruler or the authority a ruler exercises. The word bears a hierarchical sense. In fact, it's from *archon* that we get our words hier*archy,* mon*archy,* olig*archy,* etc. *Archōn* is also used to describe the "ruler" or "prince" of this world, referring to the devil (John 12:31; 14:30; 16:11; Ephesians 2:2). In addition, it's used for military rulers, political rulers and synagogue rulers. What's interesting, though, is that this word is never used in association with leaders in the New Testament church. Elders, bishops, shepherds and servants (or deacons if you like, which is an adaptation of the word for "servant" in Greek: *diakonos*)—these were the titles given to men and women who exercised authority in the church. What's more, this authority appeared to be exercised by multiple leaders of equal rank in the same fellowships. And the power used by elders in the church was expressed with the Greek word *proistēmi* rather than a derivative of the hierarchical word *archōn. Proistēmi* has the sense of maintaining, presiding over or standing before rather than the sense of commanding in a top-down way.

The authority described in the New Testament church was more akin to the Old Testament judges than the chief executives that many churches have installed as their senior pastor. Like with the nation of Israel, leadership was shared and concerned with the well-being of the community. The only leader in the church of whom the word *archōn* is used is Jesus Christ: for "God exalted him at his right hand as Leader *[archegos]* and Savior" (Acts 5:31).

God clearly meant for leadership and authority among his people to look radically different than it does in the MONOPOLY™

kingdom. "You know that the rulers in this world lord it over their people, and officials flaunt their authority over those under them," Jesus told his disciples in Matthew 20:25-27 (NLT). "But among you it will be different. Whoever wants to be a leader among you must be your servant, and whoever wants to be first among you must become your slave."

Frank Viola states in his book *Reimagining Church,* "In the Gentile world, leaders operate on the basis of a political, chain-of-command social structure—a graded hierarchy. In the kingdom of God, leadership flows from childlike meekness and sacrificial service."[3] Paul describes this kind of leadership as he writes to the Thessalonians.

As you know and as God is our witness, we never came with words of flattery or with a pretext for greed; nor did we seek praise from mortals, whether from you or from others, though we might have made demands as apostles of Christ. But we were gentle among you, like a nurse tenderly caring for her own children. So deeply do we care for you that we are determined to share with you not only the gospel of God but also our own selves, because you have become very dear to us. (1 Thessalonians 2:5-8)

Perhaps meekness, submission and obedience were such critical qualities for those within the church because the exercise of authority was to be undertaken without the threat of sword or imprisonment used by other rulers. Leadership in the church didn't imply endowing leaders with wealth and worldly status either (1 Peter 5:1-3). Authority in the church had a radically different nature than authority in the world; church leaders were undershepherds of Christ, not leading with muscle and arrogance, but leading as Jesus did, by laying down their lives.

This doesn't mean the authority invested in church leaders was optional, to be obeyed only if people liked what they had to say.

For leaders to lead without threat and without ego, followers needed to exercise humility and obedience. The writer of Hebrews urges readers, "Obey your leaders and submit to them, for they are keeping watch over your souls and will give an account" (Hebrews 13:17).

Leaders are good and necessary for the health of the church. In fact, the more I ponder the idea of meekness and submission, the more I grow convinced of the need for strong leaders.

THE BABY IN THE BATHWATER

When I set out on this project I had hoped to write a critique of the Christian infatuation with leadership. I wanted to draw our attention away from the task of leadership and onto the art of followership. But as I look back over this material, I think I have accidentally written a book about leadership.

I hope I've raised at least a few concerns about our over-indulgence of a leadership culture that has come to us from the for-profit, expansionist, superstar mindset which so easily caters to selfish ambition, biggering at any cost and an entitlement spirit. This sort of climate makes submission, meekness and a slave mindset extremely difficult to celebrate. But after more than a year of writing and thinking about all this, I have to admit: there's a baby in that leadership bathwater somewhere.

In the beautiful irony that only God can engineer, a few weeks after signing the contract for this book (which I suggested be titled *Leadership Schmeadership*), my boss, vice president of missions Jim Tebbe, said that InterVarsity's president, Alec Hill, and a few of the other VPs wondered if I might consider applying for a senior position that included oversight of InterVarsity's leadership development activities. I had to laugh internally as I turned him down; I was still too much in love with the little corner of the organization that I have labored in since my first day on the job more than twenty years ago. I have never really been drawn to the quest for more authority and more responsibility.

A week later, Jim came back and asked if I would at least pray about entering into the process. Since I was writing on the beauty of obedience, and since saying no to prayer felt wrong somehow, I decided to take him up on it. So I prayed about it and I talked to Janine. It seemed to us as though God might want to speak to me in the act of applying. Besides, the ordeal could turn into a really funny story to tell. You know . . . the guy who writes a book critiquing the cult of leadership becomes the leadership cult leader. There was just too much potential.

I met with Alec to go over the details of applying and interviewing for the position. He told me that I couldn't approach this process out of sheer obedience; I had to really want the job. It would not give him and others a fair picture of the possibilities if I were only going through the motions. To judge if I were right for this, there needed to be passion, born out of true desire for the job. He wanted to know if I was willing to give myself emotionally to the process.

This story was getting less funny. I could see only two outcomes. Number one: I get the position and have to leave a job I'm good at and people I love working with for a job that's over my head with many challenging demands. Or, number two: I don't get the job after having deliberately cultivated a passion for it, and must get reexcited about an area of student ministry that may feel old, tired and smaller than that "other job" which is so much more cosmopolitan and influential.

I decided to take Alec's advice because I trust him and the other VPs. Alec and Jim both believed that the process of pursuing this position would contribute to my growth. Besides, I was writing about submission and obedience, and it felt lame to write it but not to live it. This invitation was a request from my supervisors which I felt I should undertake seriously and with respect to their authority.

So I dreamed and ruminated. I drew up plans, and I talked to the people who surrounded this position. I laid awake at night thinking about how I could advance the kingdom of God in fresh ways through the departments and highly gifted people under this senior-level post. I got excited about this position. Really excited.

And in the end, I did not get the job.

There was disappointment, and the inevitable feelings of rejection. But I am made of fairly rubbery stuff, so it didn't take too long before I was bouncing along with fresh dreams about the area of ministry with which I have had such a long romance.

The combination of being asked to involve myself at an emotional level with a senior leadership position while undertaking a writing project that decried the dangers of allowing our leadership-laden culture to invade a kingdom where meekness, submission and obedience are most highly praised was seismic for me. Those two gigantic plates rubbed against one another and began to shake things up, and it was the juxtaposition of these events that helped me to find the baby in the bathwater, and begin to really fear (in the sense of reverent respect) the gift of leadership.

The exercise of authority is a beautiful and dangerous thing. It can produce synergy or division; it can hasten the advance or decline of communities and organizations; and we almost instinctively know when we are being well led or poorly led. A friend who works in academia tells me that most of the professors he knows love to pontificate at length about the idiots in authority positions above them, but when it comes to actually assuming authority, none of them would dare step into that place of responsibility. It is safer to complain about leaders than to lead with sobriety and meekness.

PRACTICALLY LEADING

I gather yearly with the heads of four agencies that place men and women alongside the poor in order to bring solidarity, hope and the love of Jesus: Word Made Flesh, Servant Partners, InnerCHANGE and Servants to Asia's Urban Poor. In 2006 I wrote a book to celebrate and honor the work these communities were doing, comparing them to the Frarcisans and Celtic monks and nuns. I like to refer to them as "new friars" despite the fact that there are also significant differences with Catholic orders. When I told them about this book, my friend Craig Greenfield, international coordinator for Servants to Asia's Urban Poor, responded, "That's funny. You're writing about a leadership-crazed culture, and I can't find anyone willing to step up to the plate to really lead." The others nodded in agreement. Despite the cult of leadership in the Western church, very few of the "new friars" in these fellowships aspire to lead in areas where leadership is really needed. Maybe it has something to do with the fact that their communities tend to attract those who are content just to walk alongside sex workers, street kids and slum dwellers. Two of the four organizations have the word *servant* in their name; why should they expect type-A personalities to sign up?

After my meeting with the "new friars," however, I began to think about the leadership needs in their communities and in our churches and about how little real, unabashed leadership is exercised in these contexts. Despite how readily we complain about our leaders or laugh at the submissive, SpongeBob-like followers, most of us really want to submit to people who take leadership seriously and lead with a profound understanding that they will answer to God for their leadership decisions. We want to come under meek leaders, destined to inherit the earth because they lead with love, are mindful of the powerless and feel the spiritual weight of their position.

God has given humans the gift of authority, leadership, power and dominion for the purpose of protecting the weak and advancing the common good, yet more than a third of our planet is trapped in desperate poverty. There are 165 million children as young as five years old who have been forced to work out of desperation.[4] There are more ten-year-old sex-workers than we care to imagine, and thousands are dying daily of things like diarrhea. Untold tons of grain lay rotting in warehouses while people starve to death.[5] Why does there seem to be so little order in our world, so little significant progress benefiting all, especially the "least of these"? It is because the world lacks meek leaders, leaders who exercise authority with love and are backed by the rest of us giving them our thoughtful submission.

For some who possess the gift of leadership, including me, the authority needed to lead is feared—not in the respectful sense, but in the cowardly sense. I resist exercising the kind of leadership that is born of meekness and love yet is strong, clear and unapologetic. I fear presiding over people who are willing to give me their submission because I don't want to make a mistake, or offend them by asking them to do something they don't want to do. But meek leaders don't mind offending because they're not out to build their ego. The reason I don't want to lead with strength and love is because meek leadership is not safe.

If the solution to releasing earth-inheriting, meek leadership were a good book or a conference, then the problem would have been solved decades ago. But implicit in the existence of tens of thousands of leadership books, and sometimes explicit in their content, is that we all *ought* to be leaders. This is a watered-down version of leadership. In our lust to bring out the leader in everybody we may have robbed leadership from the few who really should possess it and undermined the calling of all of us to submit. Why not identify meek people who actually have the gift of leadership, invest them with real power and then follow them with all our hearts? If the meek are going to inherit the earth anyway, we may as well start letting them do it now, giving them our obedience.

THE NEED TO AVOID

Though I believe I have the gift of leading, one of the things that prevents me from exercising strong, clear leadership with all humility is my need to be liked, a condition which meek leaders are not so concerned about because the ego of the meek is at rest.

Passivity is another trait which impairs my leadership calling. The Enneagram is a personality measuring tool based on your chief sin. My type, "the nine," struggles with sloth, or the need to avoid. In other words, that sound the car is making will probably go away if you just stop listening to it, and those concerns about an area you oversee will work themselves out eventually if you pretend they don't exist. Nines on the Enneagram have given us such memorable leaders as Dan Quayle and Gerald Ford. No, he wasn't the guy who mass-produced the automobile; that was Henry. *Rolling Stone* magazine says Gerald Ford was the most forgettable president since Millard Fillmore. (Millard who? I'll bet he was a nine.) Ask any of the people who have worked for me whether they were ever consciously aware of my rebukes and criticisms of their work. After they stop laughing, they'll say no. Whenever I screwed up the courage to bring a shortcoming to their attention, they seemed to leave the conversation feeling better about themselves and their performance. This may have the illusion of meek leadership, but in reality, the meek leader is so jealous to see justice worked out and so unaffected by what others think of him or her that confrontation—the sort Jesus exercised in the Gospels—is awakened in the meek when things aren't right.

But since beginning to think and write about meekness and submission, I've started to become more unapologetic in my leadership. Romans 12:8 says, "If God has given you leadership ability, take the responsibility seriously" (NLT). And, assuming that being a leader is at least as weighty as being a teacher, James has wise words for us as well: "Not many of you should become teachers, my brothers and sisters, for you know that we who teach will be judged with greater strictness" (James 3:1). Similarly, Paul cautions Timothy not to ordain anyone hastily (1 Timothy 5:22), because he's aware of how grave a thing it is to lead others. Jesus said that if the blind lead the blind they will all end up in deep trouble. I have become more and more afraid (in the respectful sense) of trifling with leadership. If I have the gift, and I believe I do, then I need to lead those who offer me their submission with clarity, strength, love and meekness. I need to lead as one who will give an account.

INTELLIGENT OBEDIENCE, INTELLIGENT COMMAND

Thomas Merton said, "Only someone who has himself really learned to obey intelligently is capable of assuming intelligent command."[6] Jesus exercised intelligent obedience to his Father, taking great care to obey the spirit of the law but understanding intuitively when the law had been fulfilled and could be transcended. He exercised intelligent obedience when he pleaded with the Father for a change in the course of events as the weight of the cross bore down on his soul, yet he did not waver in giving his absolute and trusting submission when it came to obeying the Father's will, even at the cost of his life. When God's will differed from his own, he declared "not my will but yours be done." This is the picture of meekness, love, leadership and power. It is what I think Merton means by intelligent obedience and intelligent command. Jesus' asking the Father for another option, eventually submitting to him, even submitting to frail and broken humanity, earned him the right to exercise intelligent command born of meekness and love.

Chris Heuertz, international executive director of Word Made Flesh, is type eight on the Enneagram—that's the "need to be against" personality. He does not have trouble with confrontation and uses his prophetic voice to question things which may be long and dearly held traditions. I have only ever seen him in shorts, a T-shirt, a hoodie and flip-flops, which pretty much defines his entire wardrobe. So when he showed up to speak at a conservative Christian college which requires students to adhere to a strict dress code, there was not a little concern and consternation on the part of the dean of the chapel. While Chris was able to take out his various earrings to speak that morning, the rest of his ensemble did not go over very well despite the fact that they were some of the best clothes he owned.

After his talk he expressed to the flustered dean that he meant no disrespect. In fact, the next day he was teaching on submission in chapel and offered to go into town to buy acceptable clothes in order to submit to their dress code. Chris writes,

> The dean brightened up at the suggestion and asked, "Would you like to do that?" I looked at him and said, "I wouldn't *like* to do that, but I'm willing to do that." I went on to explain that most of my friends around the world can't "dress up" to be accepted in places of worship, but I would do whatever was necessary for their voices to be heard through the things I came to say. The dean looked at me and, in sincere humility, thanked me for coming and told me that he was fine with the clothes I had.[7]

Chris does not mind being in the midst of controversy and loves a healthy debate, questioning things assumed to be sacred. But when it comes down to it, Chris is willing to submit if it means being heard. As a result, the communities over which Chris exercises authority know they can challenge Chris on his ideas or plans, but ultimately they will follow him because he has demonstrated the ability to carry out intelligent obedience himself.

As Christians we often readily set aside the clear commandment to love one another because we believe that the issue we are ready to draw blood over is a matter of justice. The true issue of injustice is demonstrated in our hatred and divisiveness. Perhaps we have taken too many of our leadership cues from the MONOPOLY™ kingdom. Leaders in the MONOPOLY™ kingdom lead by outranking, coercing, bribing or threatening subordinates. They guard their power and often seek to consolidate it in a quest for greater control or status. If underlings in the MONOPOLY™ kingdom don't like the way they are led, then they quit their jobs to start competing organizations in the hope that they will drive their former employer out of business. Or perhaps they'll seek to get into the office or position of the person with whom they don't agree so that they can do things their way—the "right" way.

But what works in business or politics cannot work in the kingdom of a servant Savior, at least not without changing the nature of that kingdom and converting it into a worldly one. Leadership in Jesus' kingdom is not driven by personality cult or a quest for consolidated power but through a plurality of leaders who are marked by meekness and their ability to rule with the vulnerable in mind. Obedience and submission in this kingdom are not forced but offered freely, sometimes after question and debate, but nonetheless voluntary, even when there is disagreement with those in authority. Love trumps the sense of being right.

When we submit ourselves to a servant Savior as the ultimate authority, we are able to entrust to him those called to lead, so that after appropriate testing and discussion, we can concern ourselves with following well.

CONCLUSION:
HOW TO INHERIT THE EARTH

Three friends fell in to a slightly morbid discussion of their funerals. "When I die," the first friend announced, "I want people to say, 'he was a great humanitarian!'" The second friend looked at the other two and said, "When I die, I want people to say, 'he was a great father and husband!" Finally, the two who had voiced their hopes for certain eulogies about their life on earth looked at the third friend and asked, "What about you? What do you want people to say at your funeral?" The third friend thought a moment and said, "At my funeral I want people to say, 'Look! He's moving!'"

To pursue Christ as lover, friend, confidant and commander is damning to the powers of this world, and it will not always grant you the praise of people, but when I die, I would rather be raised than praised. In the great hymn of humility penned by Paul in his letter to the Philippians, he said that because Jesus emptied himself of his God-status, took on the status and nature of a slave, and walked out submission and obedience to the point of being wrongfully executed, God exalted him. Later, Paul told Timothy that if we die with Christ we will also live with him, and if we endure hardship, we will reign with him (2 Timothy 2:11-12). The hardship Paul spoke of is a hardship produced when servants love an invisible king and meekly carry his kingdom within them, living it out in the MONOPOLY™ kingdom. There is offense, ridicule, even persecution when we live in deference to a king whose rule supersedes the rule of any earthly authority. Worldly power dynamics are confounded when the love of God shows up on earth.

There is both a "here and now" reality to the kingdom of God and a "there and then" reality. When Jesus was questioned about the source of his authority over demons, he said, "If I am casting out demons by the Spirit of God, then the Kingdom of God has arrived among you" (Matthew 12:28 NLT). Still, even though the kingdom has indeed arrived among us, there is a measure of incompleteness. Several of Jesus' parables described a king who went on a journey and left servants in charge. Some executed his just kingdom rule well while others did not. Ultimate and complete kingdom justice did not come until the king returned.

We are in that space between the heavenly Emancipation Proclamation when the oppressed are legally released from their bondage and the period of civil war and civil rights when that reality is hammered out until the arrival of the True King. Pia, Dara and others are laying aside the quest for money, status and power with the conviction that the only people to be raised up to reign at the end of the game will be those who chose not to forfeit their soul for MONOPOLY.™ They have set out on the path of the meek.

If we want to flourish spiritually, and if we want to bring the kingdom of God on earth and subvert the game of MONOPOLY™ which imprisons the poor, broken and needy while rewarding the greedy and corrupt, then we will need to set out on the path that those who will inherit the earth walk, cultivating a life that is defined by

- **meekness,** which teaches us to become like children and to embrace the downward journey at the expense of our pride

- **submission,** which doesn't shrink back from dying to self in order to subordinate our wills out of love for Christ and one another

- **repentance,** proved by the way we spin our resources out to the thirsty places in the kingdom

- **following,** our call no matter what the person next to us says or does

- **slavery,** which grants us the privilege of becoming like Jesus, who exchanged the robe of a king for the towel of a slave and in so doing killed entitlement

- **obedience,** even to fallible leaders, because independence is a sign that we are adrift

This way of meekness is natural, in the sense that it's part of our nature, but it's not easy. Becoming like a child in a culture that begs me to look grown up and important feels like taking a step downward. Dying the death of submission in a world that rewards those who seize control feels foolhardy. Giving away money to those who are in need now means I have to trust God that I'll have all I need for the future. It is difficult to follow Jesus in a calling that others are better qualified to accomplish or that requires me to sacrifice something that Jesus doesn't seem to be requiring my friends to sacrifice. And adopting the attitude of a slave means I must set self aside day after day. Finally, obeying people I perceive to be inferior or whom I simply don't want to obey means that I tie myself to others when I would rather worship freedom and independence. These are painful deaths to die. But they enrich the soil in which good things grow.

With true meekness also comes responsible leadership. When my nature urges me to please others at all costs, I must lead with conviction, knowing that meek leadership will often offend the powerful. When I would just as soon be a consultant, giving advice which can be taken or left, I need to awaken the courage to call those under me to costly obedience. And when comparison with others begs me to bigger the ministry, I must be ready to die as a mustard seed in order to achieve the right kind of success.

I am learning how to lead with the trepidation of knowing that I will give an account, and I am learning to submit with the conviction that dying to my preferences produces something far more valuable than having my way ever could. And one day when the meek inherit the earth, I hope to have died fully enough to be raised and reigning with them.

NOTES

Chapter 1: Subverting MONOPOLY™ Through Meekness
[1]A pseudonym.

[2]Adrian Levy and Cathy Scott-Clark, "Country for Sale," accessed on February 28, 2009, at <http://www.guardian.co.uk/world/2008/apr/26/cambodia>.

[3]Hernando de Soto Polar, *The Mystery of Capital* (New York: Basic Books, 2000).

[4]Gordon D. Fee and Douglas K. Stuart, *How to Read the Bible for All Its Worth: A Guide to Understanding the Bible,* 2nd ed. (Grand Rapids: Zondervan, 1993), p. 148.

[5]YWAM stands for Youth With A Mission <www.ywam.org>.

[6]A pseudonym.

Chapter 2: Meekness and the Death of Pride
[1]Dave Andrews, *Plan Be: Be the Change You Want to See in the World* (Carlisle, U.K.: Authentic Media, 2008), p. 22.

[2]It's quite likely that the questions surrounding Mary's pregnancy branded Jesus as a bastard in the eyes of everyone in his town. Village girls in honor/shame cultures who got pregnant out of wedlock and then raised their child in that same small town did not usually escape their reputation.

[3]From "How to Succeed in 2007," Business 2.0, accessed on February 3, 2009, at <http://money.cnn.com/popups/2006/biz2/howtosucceed/index.html>.

[4]Henri Nouwen, *Letters to Marc About Jesus: Living Spiritually in a Material World* (San Francisco: HarperSanFrancisco, 1985), p. 47.

Chapter 3: Submission in Our Leadership-Infatuated Culture
[1]In retrospect, leading that trip would have made it a challenging summer for my family and would have deprived the leader who took my place of an important step in her growth.

[2]With a significantly smaller body of text I had to expand my search by using the more common *lead* and *follow* instead of *leader* and *follower*. In fact, the word *follower* was not typically used at all in the Bible. *Disciple* was the more common term used to describe someone who followed, and it outnumbers the use of the word *leader* nearly twenty to one!

[3]Paul Danos, "Paul Danos, Tuck School of Business at Dartmouth College, on Mother Teresa," *Financial Times,* May 16, 2005, accessed July 26, 2008, at <http://www.ft.com/cms/s/2/9f7f6254-01dd-11db-a141-0000779e2340,dwp_

uuid=ff580540-01cf-11db-a141-0000779e2340.html>.

[4]Check out the number of references to "church" in the Gospels (in the NRSV) as compared with "kingdom." Jesus was not about making churches but rather making disciples and bringing a kingdom.

[5]Yann Martel, *Life of Pi* (Orlando, Fla.: Harcourt, 2001), p. 54.

[6]Will O'Brien, quoted in Shane Claiborne, *The Irresistible Revolution* (Grand Rapids: Zondervan, 2006), p. 164.

Chapter 4: Repentance and the Death of Personal Wealth

[1]David Thomson, *Blueprint to a Billion: 7 Essentials to Achieve Exponential Growth* (Hoboken, N.J.: John Wiley & Sons, 2006), p. 14.

[2]See the Jubilee Laws outlined in Leviticus 25.

[3]See Deuteronomy 15.

[4]When calling those confessing their sins to bear fruit worthy of repentance, John the Baptist said, "Do not begin to say to yourselves, 'We have Abraham as our ancestor'; for I tell you, God is able from these stones to raise up children to Abraham" (Luke 3:8). Jewish heritage was not enough to keep one out of torment upon death.

[5]Jesus refers to both "the least of these who are members of my family" (Matthew 25:40) and simply "the least of these" (v. 45) in this parable. Some have suggested this means that Jesus is directing our compassionate care exclusively to those followers who have suffered for their belief in him. However, Jesus' compassion was indiscriminately given to all who needed it—Jew, Gentile or Samaritan. He did not quiz them on whether they had accepted him as their Lord and Savior before feeding or healing them. And his teachings do not encourage withholding care from nonbelievers. The reference to "members of my family" may simply be Jesus utilizing another kind of "Son of Man" terminology. He often used terms like that to express his connection with the entire human race and not only those who follow him.

Chapter 5: Following and the Death of Comparison

[1]My kids would object to describing our life as "middle class" having never subscribed to cable TV or NetFlix! Our choices to live simply or have other non-family members living with us sometimes make the "middle class" label a bit of a misfit. Still, our existence is far closer to the insular suburbanite than it is to the very poor.

[2]There are some reasonable questions as to whether "the disciple whom Jesus loved" really was John or not. One theory is that this unnamed disciple was Lazarus. If so, some of my "build up" regarding the rivalry between John and Peter may not apply. Still, Peter would be engaged in comparison with another disciple in a way that detracted from his faithful followership.

[3]I doubt that first-century Judaism would have looked much different to

those of us in the West than Islam does to us today. The early church continued to practice many aspects of orthodox Judaism while remaining faithful to Christ. It's clear, for instance, that the Pharisee sect remained intact while existing within the church (Acts 15:5). Paul likely retained the garb and identity of a Pharisee while he moved from synagogue to synagogue, calling men and women to embrace Jesus as Messiah. In fact, he was still considered a Pharisee oppressor by some even after he converted (Acts 9:26), and he took on the Old Testament nazirite vow on a couple of occasions (Numbers 6:1-21; Acts 18:18; 21:23-26). I'll bet that, to the early Christians, the outward forms of a Muslim lifestyle would appear quite normal and our lifestyles as Western Christians would seem abominable. All of this to say that there are aspects of the outward forms of Islam which are perfectly consistent with first-century Christianity. Why shouldn't a few brave believers, willing to be ostracized, look for ways that Jesus might be integrated into Islamic forms, just as he has been integrated into the Western pagan forms that have come to be normal to Western Christians?

Chapter 6: Slavery and the Death of Entitlement

[1]F. F. Bruce, *Paul, Apostle of the Heart Set Free* (Grand Rapids: Eerdmans, 1977), p. 50.
[2]Some followers had left the sex trade, but to the pious that probably wouldn't have mattered much.
[3]See 2 Corinthians 10:10; 11:1-33 as well as 1 Corinthians 4:10-13.
[4]Craig S. Keener, *The IVP Bible Background Commentary: New Testament* (Downers Grove, Ill.: InterVarsity Press, 1993), p. 414; and Arthur A. Rupprecht, "Slave, Slavery," in *Dictionary of Paul and His Letters*, ed. Gerald F. Hawthorne, Ralph P. Martin and Daniel G. Reid (Downers Grove, Ill.: InterVarsity Press, 1993), pp. 881-83.
[5]For more on this, see Michael Card's *A Better Freedom: Finding Life as Slaves of Christ* (Downers Grove, Ill.: IVP Books, 2009).
[6]Scott Bessenecker, *The New Friars: The Emerging Movement Serving the World's Poor* (Downers Grove, Ill.: IVP Books, 2006), p. 152.
[7]Some translations have added the word "only," as in "look not *only* to your own interests." However, the word "only" does not appear in the Greek text.
[8]Card, *Better Freedom*, p. 52.
[9]Gregory Boyd, *The Myth of a Christian Nation: How the Quest for Political Power Is Destroying the Church* (Grand Rapids: Zondervan, 2005), p. 163.
[10]Walter Wink, *Engaging the Powers* (Minneapolis: Fortress Press, 1992), p. 142.
[11]Vast Roman armies were constantly on the move over great distances. They were expected to press civilians into service to carry their supplies,

but laws limited their ability to force civilians to carry their equipment more than a mile. For more on this see Wink, *Engaging the Powers,* pp. 179-82.

[12]Wink, *Engaging the Powers,* p. 67.

[13]John Howard Yoder, *The Politics of Jesus* (Grand Rapids: Eerdmans, 1972), p. 212.

[14]Coptic is an ancient Egyptian form of Christianity close to the Catholic and Orthodox expressions of the faith.

Chapter 7: Obedience and the Death of Independence

[1]Mother Teresa, *Mother Teresa: Come Be My Light: The Private Writings of the "Saint of Calcutta,"* ed. Brian Kolodiejchuk, M.C. (Doubleday: New York, 2007), p. 44.

[2]Ibid., p. 49.

[3]Ibid., pp. 34-35.

[4]Ibid., p. 82.

[5]*Rule* of St. Benedict, chapter 5 <www.osb.org/rb/text/toc.html#toc>.

[6]Thomas of Celano, *Vita Secunda* 152, quoted by Timothy Conway, "Saint Francis of Assisi," accessed September 29, 2009, at <www .enlightened-spirituality.org/support-files/francis_of_assisi.pdf>.

[7]Rule of Benedict, chapter three.

[8]Summa Theologica IIa IIae Q. 104, A.5

[9]Thomas Merton, *A Search for Solitude: Pursuing the Monk's True Life,* ed. Lawrence S. Cunningham, The Journals of Thomas Merton, vol. 3 (San Francisco: HarperSanFrancisco, 1996), p. 343.

[10]Ibid., p. 313.

[11]Thomas Merton, *New Seeds of Contemplation* (New York: New Directions, 2007), p. 194.

[12]From a prayer letter to supporters.

[13]From the "Servant Partners Introduction," accessed on September 20, 2008, at <http://servantpartners.org/display.php?slug=core-values>.

Chapter 8: Meekness and the Need for True Leadership

[1]Quoted in Sam Moffett, *A History of Christianity in Asia, Volume 1: Beginnings to 1500* (San Francisco: HarperSanFrancisco, 1992), p. 174.

[2]See <http://news.bbc.co.uk/2/hi/middle_east/7718587.stm>.

[3]Frank Viola, *Reimagining Church* (Colorado Springs: David C. Cook, 2008), p. 157.

[4]International Labour Organization, "Child labour," accessed on September 24, 2008, at <http://www.ilo.org/global/Themes/Child_ Labour/lang--en/index.htm>.

[5]Amitabha Bhattasali, "India's Lost Food Keeps Millions Hungry," One World South Asia, accessed on September 24, 2008, at <http://

southasia.oneworld.net/todaysheadlines/indias-lost-food-keeps-millions-hungry>.

[6]Thomas Merton, *New Seeds of Contemplation* (New York: New Directions, 2007), p. 197.

[7]Chris Heuertz, *Simple Spirituality: Learning to See God in a Broken World* (Downers Grove, Ill.: InterVarsity Press, 2008), p. 24.

LIKEWISE. *Go and do.*

A man comes across an ancient enemy, beaten and left for dead. He lifts the wounded man onto the back of a donkey and takes him to an inn to tend to the man's recovery. Jesus tells this story and instructs those who are listening to "go and do likewise."

Likewise books explore a compassionate, active faith lived out in real time. When we're skeptical about the status quo, Likewise books challenge us to create culture responsibly. When we're confused about who we are and what we're supposed to be doing, Likewise books help us listen for God's voice. When we're discouraged by the troubled world we've inherited, Likewise books encourage us to hold onto hope.

In this life we will face challenges that demand our response. Likewise books face those challenges with us so we can act on faith.

likewisebooks.com